*Focus on Hinduism
and Buddhism*

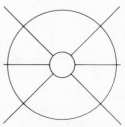

*Robert A. McDermott
Series Editor*

The Buddha is reported once to have
come before his assembled community of followers and, instead of his
usual discourse, simply stood before
them holding a lotus-flower, a smile
on his gentle face. The vision of the
Buddha thus awakened in at least
one of his disciples the "knowledge"
not only of the nature of the flower
but also of the Buddha and of his
own self. This "silent sermon," is
depicted here. It testifies to a venerable Buddhist tradition of learning
by seeing, of reaching understanding
through the medium of visual experience. It is appropriate that this depiction grace this volume on audio-
visual aids for use in learning more
about the nature of Buddhist experience.

Drawing by K. S. Ramu, Madras

FOCUS ON
BUDDHISM

A Guide to
Audio-Visual Resources
For Teaching Religion

Reviewers
  Richard B. Pilgrim
  Frederick J. Streng
  Donald K. Swearer
  Robert A. F. Thurman

Consultants
  John Ross Carter
  H. Daniel Smith

Editor, Robert A. McDermott
Associate Editor, David J. Dell

ANIMA BOOKS, 1981

Focus on Buddhism.

Bibliography: p.
Filmography: p.   Includes index.
    1. Buddhism — Audio-visual aids — Catalogs. I. McDermott, Robert A.
BQ158.5.F63   016.2943   81-8084
ISBN 0-89012-020-X   AACR2
ISBN 0-89012-021-8 (pbk.)

    This volume is part of a series of guides to the audio-visual materials useful
for the study of Hinduism and Buddhism. Preparation and publication of
these volumes were made possible by a grant from the National Endowment
for the Humanities to the Council on International and Public Affairs, Inc.
(Ward Morehouse, President), with Robert A. McDermott, Project Director.
Through the Endowment's provision for matching funds, this project was also
supported by the Ada Howe Kent Foundation, Baruch College, CUNY, the
NDEA Center fr South Asian Studies at Columbia University, the Standing
Committee on the Study of World Philosophies and Religions (Robert A.
McDermott, Chairman) of the Council for Intercultural Studies and
Programs.

Printed in USA.

ANIMA BOOKS is a subdivision of Conococheague Associates, Inc., 1053
Wilson Avenue, Chambersburg, Pennsylvania 17201.

Contents

Preface

THIS GUIDE to films, slide sets, and recordings for the study of Buddhism is intended for anyone seeking to understand the history, teachings, practices, and cultural background of the Buddhist religious tradition. It is both the latest in a series of publications seeking to strengthen the study of Asian religions and philosophies, as well as the first of a series of publications specifically concerning the audio-visual materials useful for the study of Buddhism as a religious tradition. All of these efforts were made possible by the initiatives of Kenneth W. Morgan and Ward Morehouse, and by the generous support of the National Endowment for the Humanities.

The Project to Strengthen Undergraduate Teaching in Asian Philosophies and Religions (1971-77), which has produced a seven-volume annotated bibliographical guide for Asian philosophies and religions (publication by G. K. Hall, forthcoming), was supported by a grant from the National Endowment for the Humanities to the Council for Intercultural Studies and Programs (Ward Morehouse, President). Subsequently, as a complement to these bibliographies, Ward Morehouse formed a committee for the review of audio-visual materials for the study of Hinduism, again with the support of NEH. This project produced *Focus on Hinduism*, published in 1977 by the Foreign Area Materials Center and the Council for Intercultural Studies and Programs, and recently revised and published in this series as a companion volume to the present work.

The entire project was a collaborative effort. Almost every film was viewed by at least three specialists in Buddhist studies, including at least two of the four principal authors. The specialized scholarship of the four principal authors—Professors Pilgrim, Streng, Swearer, and Thurman—roughly correspond to the main cultural areas of historical and contemporary Buddhism. Each of these authors assumed a special responsibility for the films (and to some extent, the slides) in his scholarly area:

Frederick J. Streng: Indian Buddhism and General/Historical Introductions.

As an accomplished historian of religions and an editor of a multivolumed introduction to Asian religions, Professor Streng was able to evaluate these films from the perspective of the history of Buddhism. All of the other three specialists serve as second and third reviewers for these historical and introductory films.

Donald K. Swearer: Southeast Asian and Theravada Buddhism.
All of the films on Buddhism in Southeast Asia, as well as other films which emphasize Theravada Buddhist theory and practice, fell within the special competence of Dr. Swearer. Bardwell L. Smith (Carleton College), an expert on Theravada Buddhism, joined the other three specialists as second and third reviewers.

Robert A. F. Thurman: Tibetan and Chinese.
As principal reviewer of all films on China and Tibet, Professor Thurman was joined by the other three specialists, as well as by David Dell. The enthusiasm for things Tibetan which characterized many of the reviews of Tibetan Buddhist films can safely be ascribed to Professor Thurman's informed and articulate love for Tibet.

Richard B. Pilgrim: Japanese Buddhism.
Professor Pilgrim was principally responsible for the enormous group of films on Japanese Buddhism, including a large group of films on Zen. Professor Pilgrim's influence can be discerned in the sensitive (and perhaps occasionally controversial) emphasis of the Buddhist (and particularly Zen) influence on the arts of Japan.

David Dell:
In addition to playing a major role in every phase of the project, Dr. Dell was the primary reviewer of slide sets and recordings.
The project director is grateful to these four specialists for their consistent willingness to review these films on a rather exacting schedule, and for their acceptance of his suggestions for revision. He is also grateful to David Dell for assisting in the task of editing the entire manuscript, including the style and contents of reviews and the Topical Index.
H. Daniel Smith, who also revised and updated the second edition of *Focus on Hinduism,* has served as advisor to the entire project, and made many helpful suggestions for revision. John Ross Carter also made important suggestions for improvement.
This project has also been assisted by the following:

Ada Howe Kent Foundation, for a grant which facilitated the preparation and publication of this guide.
Columbia University South Asia Center, for use of audio-visual facilities and for office space provided for the project coordinator, David J. Dell.
Baruch College, particularly its School of Liberal Arts and Department of Philosophy, for office space, supplies, and telephone privileges.
John Carman, Director, and William Darrow, Administrative Assistant,

The Center for the Study of World Religions, Harvard University, for their many kindnesses while hosting this project during several weekends of film reviewing.

Peter Grilli, Director, Japan Society, for locating and lending for review several films on Japanese Buddhist arts produced and distributed in Japan.

Bardwell L. Smith for his contributions as a critical reviewer and generously making accessible the extensive collection of audio-visual resources of the Department of Religion, Carleton College, Northfield, Minnesota.

Elizabeth S. Rosen, Institute of Fine Arts of New York University, for aid in critical evaluation of slide sets treating Buddhist art.

The project director is grateful to Leslie Austin for her conscientious and capable assistance as researcher, cataloguer, and office manager.

Those of us who have worked on this guide for the past two years recognize that it is still imperfect. The committee welcomes suggestions for revision of this guide, particularly concerning errors, omissions, and new developments. Please address correspondence to Robert A. McDermott, Philosophy Department (Box 329), Baruch College/ CUNY, New York, NY 10010.

Finally, all of us who have worked on this project wish to express our gratitude to Professor Kenneth W. Morgan, our predecessor and inspiration in this work. Professor Morgan has long pioneered the use of audio-visual materials for the study of Asian religions, beginning with a basic slide set he developed more than twenty-five years ago, and continuing with his contribution to the previously mentioned seven-volume annotated bibliography and *Focus on Hinduism*. It is in light of these important contributions and for the leadership Professor Morgan has provided to the present generation of professors of Asian religions that this volume is gratefully dedicated to him.

Robert A. McDermott
Project Director

Rye, New York
January, 1981

Introduction: Audio-Visual Materials and Buddhism

by Robert A. McDermott

Introduction

PROFESSORS OF RELIGION, and undoubtedly many of their students as well, have long been aware of a split between professors who teach only one tradition (most commonly Christianity) and those who regularly discourse on two or more traditions. In recent years, there has emerged another similar split, that between professors who use only the written and spoken word, and those who also use audio and visual materials in undergraduate courses on religion. As is the case in the conflict between the perspective of one versus more than one tradition, the conflict between users and nonusers of A-V materials tends to produce predictable, and sometimes inflexible, reactions: to the traditional, print-oriented approach, use of audio-visual materials is often regarded as frivolous, mistaken, or perhaps threatening to sound scholarship and pedagogy; to the A-V enthusiast, the exclusive commitment to print tends to appear stubborn, parochial, and anachronistic. Obviously, these are extreme positions with the vast majority of the professors falling somewhere between the two. But the polarity, in this absolute form, helps to emphasize the very real resistance to the use of audio-visual materials on the part of many, if not most, professors of religion, and the revealing ways in which this resistance resembles the long-standing suspicion regarding the study of Asian religions in general.

Nor is it accidental that the study of Asian religions and the use of audio-visual materials should meet a similar resistance, for they each resist the established, Christian-based approach to the study of religion encapsuled in the phrase, "religion of the Book." Buddhism is remarkable for the degree to which it should be seen to be understood. Instructors in college courses on the Christian religious tradition and independent learners studying Christianity may assume—often mistakenly—a basic familiarity with Christian history, belief, and practice. No such assumption is possible, however, in the study of Asian religious traditions where the language and culture are entirely foreign and either professors nor students have experienced such religions in their indigenous contexts. Interestingly, professors who do venture into the Asian area with the aid of audio-visual materials are frequently impressed by the need for similar audio-visual materials in the study of Christianity, albeit a less urgent need then in the study of Asian religions.

While specialists and novices in the study of Asian religions might agree on the need for extensive use of audio-visual materials in order to understand vividly the lived experience of Asian religions, there remain many hurdles to the effective use of such materials. Most, if not all, of these obstacles fall within one of the following three questions:

What is available?
How does one know what to use/rent/purchase?
How can these materials be used most effectively?

This guide aims to answer the first two of these questions—availability and selection—but in the process it will also give many hints on the most effective use of films, slides, and recordings. Additional publications in this series—specifically thematic guides and model curricula—offer additional guidance on the most effective use of these materials.

In this, the first comprehensive guide to audio-visual materials for the study of Buddhism, the term *available materials* takes on a new scope and specificity. Intended for the study of Buddhism as a religious tradition, there are currently available at least 115 English language films, 30 slide sets, and numerous recordings. With this array, it is now possible to assess realistically the contents and use of these materials for the study of the Buddhist religious tradition.

Readers entirely new to the use of films may find this plethora of material more overwhelming than inviting. The only sure way to overcome this fear is to plunge—and thereby discover that the materials reviewed in these pages will ordinarily be available when you request them, will be received on time, and will be easy to use and return. A phone call to the distributor to check on prices, schedule, and mailing instructions should eliminate any lingering doubts about the process of renting and returning films.

Available Films

IN THIS VOLUME 115 films are reviewed. In addition to basic information—title, producer/director, sale/rental, distributor—each review offers a description of the contents of the film as well as evaluative comments on its usefulness. These films reveal a remarkable range of topical variety and cinematic quality. Throughout, the reviews emphasize the need for fruitful interplay between rich visual material on the one hand and conceptual and historical accuracy on the other—and the ways in which many films fail on either or both counts. The reviews explain and evaluate films within the broad context of contemporary scholarly and pedagogical developments. While this guide serves its primary function as a reference work, its authors hope that many instructors and students seriously interested in the study of Buddhism will read the entire guide, particularly the film reviews wherein an effort is made to direct the nonspecialist to films that most faithfully present the Buddhist religious tradition. Readers may well find that reviews of the weakest films will provide the most valuable insights concerning the tendency shared by viewers and film-makers alike to approach the study of Buddhism with stereotypical preconceptions.

A careful reading of the entire film section, then, will disclose not only basic information concerning the content of films on Buddhism, but will also indicate the myriad topics and approaches which may effectively be treated in courses or independent studies on the Buddhist religious tradition. This guide offers a choice of films on such varied topics as the life and teaching of the Buddha, Buddhist ritual and pilgrimage, sacred persons and places, temples and art works, and the relation of Buddhist life to contemporary secular attitudes and institutions. The Subject Index suggests the array of topics covered within these films—although admittedly the treatment of these topics in the films is all too often misleading or inadequate.

Given the international, intercultural, and highly diverse history of Buddhism, it was logical to arrange the films according to geographical/cultural areas. After a section on general/introductory films, the remaining films are classified according to the following areas: South Asia (India and Sri Lanka), Southeast Asia, Himalaya, China, Japan and Korea, and Buddhism in (or and) the West. Each of these groups of films is discussed in turn as follows:

General Introduction:
Historical Surveys and Spiritual Discipline
Since many viewers, particularly instructors in a college survey course on Asian religions, may be in search of films on an introductory level, a selection of introductory films has been placed at the front of this catalogue. Unfortunately, though perhaps understandably, there are very few first-rate films which can be regarded as offering an adequate general introduction to the Buddhist tradition. In light of the complexity of the history, beliefs, and practices of Buddhism, some specialists doubt both the possibility and desirability of such a film. Irrespective of one's position on this question, the fact remains that films that purport to be a general introduction to Buddhism tend to be far less adequate than films limited to a specific topic or cultural area. Such limitations seem to provide the focus essential for an intelligible film. For example, the two films recently produced by BBC, *Buddhism:*

Footprint of the Buddha —India and *Buddhism: Land of Disappearing Buddha—Japan,* serve equally as an introduction to Buddhism generally and to Buddhism in the Sri Lankan and Japanese contexts, respectively. While it may be possible to produce a successful comprehensive introductory film on Buddhism, most of the better films included in this introductory section tend to be focused on one culture or one aspect of Buddhism, but are at the same time (and perhaps for this reason) effective as introductions to the Buddhist religious tradition.

The specificity of such introductory films seems to fall into two broad types: the historical survey (e.g., *Buddhism in China*) or Buddhism as a spiritual discipline (e.g., *Zen in Life, I Am a Monk, The Smile*). While it may be simplistic to regard this division as the outer and inner aspects of the Buddhist tradition, something of this distinction is at work here. A few films, specifically both of the BBC films— both lengthy (52 minutes) and complex films—combine these two approaches, and thereby offer an unusually rich grasp of the Buddhist tradition. On the other hand, complexity and comprehensiveness are not necessarily merits of a film. For many purposes, an intelligent treatment of a specific topic would be more useful (e.g., *Vejen* or *The Smile*). Consequently, it would be a mistake to regard the introductory group of films as inherently more appropriate for beginning the study of Buddhism; they are grouped together to facilitate comparison and because they can be used for (and in some cases purport to be) a general introduction to Buddhism

South Asia

Since living Buddhism has not been an active force in India for nearly one thousand years, almost all of the films that treat Buddhism in India are primarily concerned with historical sites and Buddhist art. Of these, *The Glory That Remains* is perhaps the most effective general presentation, and *Immortal Stupa* is one of the more effective presentations of a single site—the remains at Sanchi—an important Buddhist pilgrimage site and center of learning from third century B.C. to Sixth century A.D.

For a view of living Buddhism in South Asia, we must look to Sri Lanka (Ceylon). Theravada Buddhism, as practiced in Sri Lanka, has been filmed effectively in *Buddhism: Footprints of the Buddha— India, Buddhism: The Path to Enlightenment,* and in a more focused way, in *Vesak.*

Southeast Asia

Of the Southeast Asian Buddhist countries—Thailand, Cambodia, Laos, Burma, and Indonesia—most of the best films are set in Thailand. *Buddhism: Be Ye Lamps Unto Yourselves, Buddhism: The Path to Enlightenment,* and *I Am a Monk,* are all excellent cinematographic introductions to Theravada Buddhism in general, and more particularly, Buddhism in the context of Thai social and cultural life. *The Smile* and *Vejen*, both very effective films on Buddhism in Burma, similarly serve as representative samples of Theravada Buddhist practice. Unfortunately, we have found no film treatments of Buddhism in Viet Nam. Films on Buddhism in Cambodia and Indonesia consist primarily in treatments of their splendid ancient monasteries and historical sites: there are two films on Angkor, the fabulous Buddhist capitol of Buddhist wats (temple complexes) in Cambodia, and two films on Borobudor, the important Buddhist monument in Java, Indonesia.

Himalayan

As a look at the Index (see under Himalaya and Tibet) will indicate, there is no shortage of films on Buddhism in this area. Many of them are visually and conceptually competent. Because much of the Tibetan religious community has been in forced exile in India since 1960, many of the films on Tibetan Buddhism treat religious traditions and practices uprooted from their original setting. Among the best of these film treatments are *A Prophecy*, *The Lama King*, and *Tantra of Gyuto*. Historical footage is available in *Out of This World: Forbidden Tibet*. Himalayan Buddhism is also seen in two films on Bhutan, *Bhutan: Land of the Peaceful Dragon* and *A King is Crowned;* in Nepal, *Tibetan Heritage* and *The Tantric Universe;* and in Kashmir, *Ladakh*.

China

With the exception of *Buddhism in China*, which serves well as an introduction to the history of Buddhism including its Indian origin and development in Tibet, virtually all of the films surveyed on Buddhism in China are limited to art-historical materials. Since it has been difficult to film Buddhism in China for the past three decades, there are no film treatments of Buddhist life or practice in the People's Republic. It is possible, however, to treat Buddhist practice in Hong Kong and Taiwan by the use of the slide set *Chinese Religions*, along with the recording *Chinese Buddhist Music*. Wang-Go Weng's Chinese History Series uses art historical materials to provide cultural history.

Japan and Korea

More than one third of the 115 films reviewed in this guide are treatments of Buddhism in Japan. There is comparatively little on Buddhism in Korea. Of the 40 films on Japanese Buddhism, approximately 10 are entirely or at least substantially concerned with the history or practices of Zen. Because of the intimate relation between Zen and Japanese culture, many of the films on Japanese arts are also treatments of Zen—although in many cases this treatment is obvious only if the viewer is aware of this relationship between Zen and the arts.

Perhaps the most useful general treatment of Buddhism in Japan is the BBC film, *Buddhism: Land of the Disappearing Buddha—Japan*. Three excellent films, *Hiraizumi...*, *Yakushiji...*, and *Torches of Todaiji*, treat traditional Japanese Buddhist temple complexes and communities. The two best films on Zen, particularly on the meaning and practice of Zen discipline, are *Zen in Life* and *Zen in Ryoko-in*.

Buddhism and the West
In a way that accurately mirrors the current enthusiasm in the West for Asian religions and spiritual disciplines, many of the films on Buddhism in the West focus on Zen meditation, both of the rather nebulous Alan Watts variety *(Art of Meditation, Buddhism, Man and Nature, Mood of Zen, Flow of Zen, Zen and Now)*, and the brief but revealing glimpse of San Francisco Zen Center, *Zen in America Empowerment* shows glimpses of the Tibetan tradition as experienced in the West, and *Cathedral of the Pines...* depicts a Chinese-American service in observance of the American Bicentennial. Perhaps the most notable of the films on Buddhism and the West are the two films listed in the introductory section: *I Am a Monk*, concerning an American who became a Buddhist novice in Thailand, and *Awareness*, an attempt to present the life of the Buddha through American imagery. The Nichiren Shoshu Academy has a number of films largely for internal consumption, chronicling the main events of its annual conventions and other activities *(New York Convention—1976* and *Pre-Bicentennial Convention in Blue Hawaii [1975])*.

Use and Acquisition of Films
Instructors experienced in the use of audio-visual materials are well aware there are many ways to use films, including films that may be seriously flawed. It can be effective, for example, to show only one section of a film (perhaps juxtaposed with footage from another film treating the same topic or supplemented by slides), or to show the visuals without the narration (either in order to concentrate better on the visual or to replace an inadequate narration). It might even be useful upon occasion to show a film replete with misinformation, misjudgements, or stereotypical opinions in order to analyze the extent to which such misperceptions are shared by the viewers. As with all teaching, the most effective use of films is greatly enhanced by a blend of painstaking preparation and an imaginative presentation.

Independent learners will discover that films will provide the sight and sound of religious experience in a way that no other medium can; but when used without the benefit of adequate preparatory knowledge, or as a substitute for knowledge of the Buddhist history, texts, and teachings, they fail to take root. It would be counter-productive for an independent learner to attempt to study Buddhism only through these films. Before viewing them, an independent viewer should at least read a solid introduction, e.g., the excellent section on Buddhist religion in *Encyclopaedia Britannica* (15th edition), Macropedia 3, pp. 369–441.

Building a Basic Film Library

Members of this committee are often asked to supply a list of absolutely indispensible films, or a beginning list for a college department or library with limited funds for purchase or rental. In response to this request, and after considerable discussion and revision, the committee has judged the following to be worthy of inclusion on any list of basic films. Together these ten films constitute what might be considered a basic library of currently available films.

General/Introductory
   Historical:
     Buddhism in China
   Spiritual Discipline:
     I Am a Monk
South Asia
   Buddhism: Footprint of the Buddha—India
Southeast Asia
   Buddhism: Be Ye Lamps unto Yourselves
   Vejen
Himalaya
   The Lama King
   Tibetan Heritage
Japan
   Buddhism: Land of the Disappearing Buddha—Japan
   Zen in Life
Buddhism in the West
   Refuge

Slides

IN ADDITION TO books and films, the third most widely and effectively used materials for the study of Buddhism are slide sets. Slides, of course, can be arranged according to one's particular approach or interest. Unlike a film (although not unlike videocassette), slides can be examined at length and detail. Obviously, they are also less expensive than films. On the negative side, however, slides require considerably more assistance in the form of written materials. Even more than is the case with films, slide sets cannot profitably be viewed without extensive preparation by the course instructor or independent viewer. Unfortunately, most of the visually excellent slides on Buddhism have been developed from the perspective of art history, with little or no treatment of religious themes. Further, these art historical slide sets— e.g., the nine sets produced by the American Committee on South Asian Art (ACSAA)—provide only minimal identification of each slide.

There is definitely a need for a good series of professionally photographed, sharply defined slide sets on Buddhism with clear accompanying notes. Mudras and mandalas used particularly in Tibetan Buddhism and in Japanese Shingon Buddhism require the cooperation of visual and conceptual modes of presentation. A slide set on the development of Buddhist architecture from the stupa to the modern temples of Japan would be useful, as would a set on the development of Buddhist iconography. Ritual implements from the begging bowl to incense and a detailed look at particular rituals would also serve a useful purpose in the study of Buddhism.

There is need for audio-visual treatments of the following: a slide set on Vesak, the Buddha's birthday as celebrated in various Buddhist countries; Buddhist cosmology; color symbolism; personal rituals; rites of passage, such as weddings and funerals; complete Jataka tales illustrated from a variety of sources; and a representative selection of arhat, siddhas, disciples, bodhisattvas, and Buddhas.

There are, however, a few sets of slides well suited to the study of religion. The pioneering survey of Buddhism by Kenneth W. Morgan remains a good starting point for any collection. This and the basic slide sets on Tibet, Southeast Asia, China, Korea, and Japan, prepared by Charles Kennedy and others for the American Academy of Religion, are available for sale or rental from Yale Audio Visual Service.

Four useful and inexpensive slide sets have been prepared by New York University Asian Studies Curriculum Center. These sets illustrate that pedagogically worthwhile materials can be produced by carefully focusing on a single theme, but they also indicate the degree to which amateur photography can interfere with an otherwise effective production. Kai-Dib has produced beautiful slides on Zen gardens, but faulty conception limits their usefulness.

Surprisingly, the series of otherwise undistinguished slides produced by Scholarly Publications includes one useful item, *Zen*, in which the practice of Zazen or sitting is adeptly portrayed in twenty-five good slides accompanied by a few short pages of notes.

Recordings

VIRTUALLY ALL OF the currently available recordings of Buddhist liturgical music are of Tibetan and Japanese music. There is only one record devoted entirely to Chinese Buddhist music, and three bands of another. A few bands on assorted albums have South Asian and Korean Buddhist music. Since Buddhist music varies greatly according to sect and country and includes a wide variety of highly developed musical styles important for different traditions of ritual, communal worship, and meditation, there is clearly a need for many more recordings of Buddhist music. In the interim, the best single introductory recording is *The Way of Eheiji*.

Recommendations to Film-makers

A postscript to the Introduction of *Focus on Hinduism* urges film-makers to consult with academic specialists concerning the conception and creation of films to be used in academic study. The concluding paragraph of this postscript is as valid for Buddhism as for Hinduism:

> The present lists with evaluations may provide the first clear evidence for those who plan, produce, distribute, and purchase films and other learning resources just what expectations classroom specialists have for learning resources focusing on Hinduism. The present statement, by way of a "Postscript" to this project, may also be the first time a call for collaboration has been issued, an invitation that is more poignant for being so long overdue.
>
> *(Focus on Hinduism, p. 13)*

More specifically, the committee of reviewers for films on Buddhism recommend that film-makers consider producing films on the following topics. These films ought to be approximately thirty minutes, and ought to have the active advice of academics who have an experienced sense of the pedagogical requirements of such films:

1. General Introduction.
Despite the extreme difficulty of this task, there is a permanent need for such a film. A successful introduction to Buddhism will surely be widely used. The committee recommends that this film include a representative selection of history, teaching, and practice; use of on-site footage; emphasis on the variety and importance of cultural diversity; a survey of the dominant forms of modern Buddhism, perhaps using Heinrich Dumoulin's *Buddhism in the Modern World* (New York: Macmillan, 1976) as a model; effective use of maps and other visual aids.

2. Mahayana Buddhism.
There is particular need for a film with an emphasis on the complexity and variety of the Mahayana sectarian tradition.

3. Buddhist Ritual.
H. Daniel Smith's *Image India: The Hindu Way* would serve as an excellent model for a film or series of films on Buddhist ritual.

4. Buddhist Pilgrimage,
preferable from a comparative or cross-cultural perspective.

5. Development of the Buddha Image,
including the development of bodhisattvas and ideal beings; preferably as a vehicle for conveying the development of Buddhist thought, not merely from an art-historical point of view.

6. Buddhism and Society.

In addition to the general need for treatments of this topic in many parts of the Buddhist world, there is a particular need to use old footage of living Buddhism in countries which in recent years have experienced cultural, political, and religious revolutions. Old footage provides an irreplaceable record of Buddhism as it once existed in these countries.

7. Lay Buddhism

8. Buddhist Meditation, Spiritual Discipline, and Teaching Techniques

Reviews of
Audio-Visual Materials

General and Historical Introductions

Films

Awareness
The Buddha
The Buddha in South Asia
Buddhism (Great Religions Series)
Buddhism (The Religions of Man)
Buddhism: Be Ye Lamps unto Yourselves
Buddhism: Footprint of the Buddha—India
Buddhism in China
Buddhism: Land of the Disappearing Buddha—Japan
Buddhism: The Path to Enlightenment
Buddhist Art
The Buddhist World
Guatama the Buddha
I Am a Monk
Mahayana Buddhism
Meditation
The Smile
Theravada Buddhism
Vejen
Zen in Life
Zen in Ryoko-in

Slides

Buddha and His Teachings
Buddhism
The Buddhist Tradition: Buddhism in Burma
The Buddhist Tradition: Buddhism in Japan
Evolution of the Buddha Image
History of the Oriental Arts
Marks and Mudras of the Buddha
Monk's Ordination Ceremony
The World's Great Religions—Buddhism

Recordings

Religious Music of Asia

Films

Awareness
  25 minutes, color, 16mm, 1968
  Sale $300.00, Rental $25.00
  Director: Rolf Forsberg
  Producer: Gil Sorenson for the University of Michigan
  Distributor: Mass Media Ministries
  Also available from: ArizSt, UMich

The film attempts to dramatize the life of the Buddha and to present his teaching through contemporary American imagery such as the use of a chauffeur-driven car, a hospital, a junk yard, and a funeral. It portrays basic Buddhist doctrine in such generalizations as: life is change, humanity creates illusion, there is no personal ego, life is full of suffering, nirvana is putting out the fire of self-centeredness, and the highest virtue is compassion for all living beings epitomized in Maitreya. This is a student-made film with students playing key character roles.

This film is a somewhat controversial and unusual presentation of the meaning of Buddhist experience. However well intentioned, the presentation—as exemplified particularly in the martial arts and tea ceremony scenes—does not indicate the mental and psychological discipline found in traditional Buddhist spiritual efforts. It suggests an oversimplified identity between spiritual insight and sensuous appreciation of life around us. Classroom use of this film is risky but may provoke lively discussion.

The Buddha
  184 minutes, color, 16mm. Out of print
  Distributor: Audio Brandon Films (discontinued)

This is the only full-length feature *in Japanese* on the life of the Buddha: it dramatizes the famous episodes of the Teacher's life with live actors, drawing eclectically from Theravada and Mahayana sources. Special effects animation is used to convey the miraculous events surrounding Siddhartha's birth, with all the trees and flowers blooming out of season, and the newborn child emitting golden halo rays as he takes his famous first steps. The scenes of his youth are treated imaginatively, and he is depicted as a sensitive and noble youth who automatically recoils against the brutalities and social inequalities of his age. The scene where he perceives the sick man, old man, corpse, and, ascetic is effectively presented, as is his renunciation of the world and the distress it causes his family. The interplay of the wicked cousin Devadatta is then exploited by the director to infuse an element of drama into the long meditation sequence, as the Prince is always restraining himself from rushing back to Kapilavastu to save the forlorn Yasodhara from the aggressive advances of Devadatta. The enlightenment is then achieved after a rather poorly staged temptation scene, where the devilish Maras are portrayed by halloween-like actors in an unsuccessful attempt at realism.

During the teaching tenure of the fully-enlightened Buddha, the wicked Devadatta story is again brought to the fore. The climax of the movie comes with the defeat of Devadatta in a sequence worthy of Hollywood at its most flamboyant. The film concludes with good established over evil, and a joyous parinirvana.

A devout Buddhist, or even an imaginative and sympathetic knower of the Buddha story could appreciate this film deeply. However, in addition to the fact that it is rather crudely dubbed in English, the real problem for an American audience is that the actors bring to the tale a quality of melodrama more appropriate to a Japanese "Samurai Western." This mars what could be powerful scenes and makes it hard going for a normal college audience. Therefore, it is not recommended for ordinary course use.

The Buddha in South Asia
   29 minutes, color, ¾″ Videocassette, 1975
   Sale $45.00, Rental none
   Director and Narrator: David M. Knipe
   Producer: John James
   Series: Exploring the Religions of South Asia
   Distributor: University of Wisconsin South Asia Center

Using an interview format, this videocassette provides basic information and an interpretation of the Buddhist traditions in India. Dr. Stephan Beyer, of the University of Wisconsin, responds to questions of series host, Dr. David M. Knipe. The lecture focuses primarily on the Three Refuges: the Buddha, Dharma, and Sangha. It summarizes the development of Indian Mahayana Buddhism, provides a brief introduction to Vajrayana, and mentions the contemporary revival of Buddhism in India under B. R. Ambedkar. During the lecture, background pictures such as scenes from Bodhgaya, the Buddha's image, and details of the Buddha's hand gestures are shown; accompanying Sanskrit terms appear at the bottom of the screen.

This is an insightful and accurate presentation. Nevertheless, some viewers might feel that Beyer talks too fast, and that too many key points are covered too quickly. More visual material of religious practice, imagery, and life could have been used—as in the video cassette "Sectarian Hinduism: Lord Siva and His Worship," also found in this series. The discussion of the difference between Theravada and Mahayana is suggestive rather than clearly articulated. The brief presentation and selection of material on Indian Buddhist Tantrism is insufficient to the point of being misleading. Overall, the cassette's complexity limits its usefulness at the introductory level, making it perhaps more appropriate as a review in an upper-level class.

Buddhism
  16 minutes, b/w, 16mm, 1962
  Sale $140.00, Rental $20.00
  Producer: James Beveridge
  Series: Great Religions
  Distributor: National Film Board of Canada
  Also available from: ArizSt, UCB, FlaSt, UIll, IowaSt, BU, UMinn, UNeb, SyrU, KentSt, PennSt, UTex, BYU, WashSt

This film opens with an account of the "Life of Gautama" depicted through selected artistic representations of the Buddha's nativity, renunciation, enlightment, etc. Next comes a section on the doctrine with emphasis on the "Four Noble Truths," visually accompanied by scenes of the great monuments of Indian Buddhism. The next section surveys Theravada Buddhism, giving a sense of its spread through Southeast Asia; most of the footage here is from Burma—a floating pagoda and a tonsure ceremony. This third part of the film emphasizes self-reliance and lack of interest in gods, stressing the normative monastic view of religion prevalent in these cultures. Finally, the Mahayana is quickly sketched in its spread to China, Central Asia, and Japan. Unfortunate stereotypes are perpetuated here, including the deplorable assertion that "demon worship" is found in Tibetan Buddhism and that the Buddha Amitabha is "God Himself." Also notable is the overemphasis on the function of the tea ceremony and on "sudden enlightment" in Japanese Buddhism.

This film is distorted by a basically apologetic approach, presenting Buddhism in terms too familiar to Westerners. It is also marred by some inaccuracies. However, the camera work is generally good, and the works of art are well chosen. It can be recommended for introductory classroom use if it is accompanied by appropriate lecture and/or reading assignments.

Buddhism
  90 minutes, b/w, 16mm, 1955
  Sale out of print, Rental $28.50
  Producer: Dr. Huston Smith for WKED-TV
  Series: The Religions of Man
  Distributor: Indiana University
  Also available from: UAriz, UCB, KentSt, BYU

This is a series of three half-hour lectures delivered by Professor Huston Smith in 1955 on WKED-TV in St. Louis. These lectures undoubtedly were epoch-making in their day, and hence of some interest in the history of the teaching of comparative religion in the United States. The interesting text of these lectures is available, with the addition of considerable information and polish, as the "Buddhism" chapter of Professor Smith's *The Religions of Man* (Harper and Row, 1958). Aside from this historical interest, however, there are no longer any remaining cinematic qualities to recommend this film for classroom or independent use.

Buddhism: Be Ye Lamps Unto Yourselves
  29 minutes, color, 16mm, 1973
  Sale $415.00, Rental $28.00
  Producer: Howard Enders for ABC
  Series : Directions
  Distributor: Xerox Films
  Also available from: UIH, UMinn, UMo

Through a focus on the present monastic life in Thailand, this film explains basic practices and teachings of Theravada Buddhism. It integrates various scenes with over-voice quo: tions from the Theravada canon and an explanatory commentary on Buddhist life. Scenes include novice ordinations in rural and urban temples, monks chanting the Buddhist teaching and meditating, lay merit-producing activities such as alms-giving and funeral rites. Interviews with monks and with Dr. Donald K. Swearer help to interpret the purpose and central concepts of Theravada.

The photography is superb and in general, the content is judiciously selected. Several points of comparison between Buddhism and Christianity are helpful for a clarification of similarities and contrasts between these religious traditions, although the claim of a Buddhist monk's independence from external guidance in attaining spiritual goals is over-emphasized. Some may find the tone of the narrator unengaging. Nevertheless, this is an effective film on contemporary Thai Buddhism and one of the best introductions to Theravada Buddhism. For introductions to Theravada which present the Buddhism of Sri Lanka, *see Buddhism: The Path to Enlightenment* and *Buddhism: Footprint of the Buddha-India.*

Buddhism: Footprint of the Buddha—India
  54 minutes, color, 16mm, 1977
  Sale $800.00, Rental $100.00
  ¾" videocassette, Sale $200.00. ½" video cassette, Sale $150.00

Narrator: Ronald Eyre
Producer: Peter Montagnon for BBC
Series: The Long Search
Distributor: Time-Life Video, Inc.

Buddhism: Footprint of the Buddha—India, one of thirteen films in The Long Search series, reveals Theravada Buddhism as a religion lived by monks and lay persons. The viewer follows a Western observer interlocutor, Ronald Eyre, on a search for the nature of Buddhism in Sri Lanka. The search journeys to the Buddha statues of Polannaruwa, the site of the Buddha's enlightenment at Bodhgaya in India an ordination ritual, monks on alms-giving rounds, a rains retreat ceremony on the May full moon sabbath day, and finally to meditating monks at the Dambulla cave monastery north of Kandy. These stops are occasions for an investigation into the nature of Theravada beliefs, teachings, and practices, including the moral precepts and the Eightfold Noble Path, the nature of the Buddha, astrology, supernatural powers, gift-giving and merit, and the nature of Buddhist mindfulness. Theravada Buddhism is characterized primarily as a journey to a higher goal achieved by ones self without reliance on any outside power of authority. It depicts this life as one moving from the poles of withdrawal/meditation to involvement/service.

In general, this film is well balanced and beautifully produced. The observer/narrator device works smoothly, helping to create an atmosphere of unhurried exploration. Only occasionally does Mr. Eyre intrude: Ananda Maitreya, the chief monastic informant, is memorable throughout. The camera sensitively captures and integrates events and conversations; transitions from one to the other are natural and logical.

This film focuses on the monastic life and the interaction between monk and laity without attempting to develop fully the cultural context and its impact on Theravada Buddhism in Sri Lanka. Appropriate for independent or classroom use, its content is richer and narration superior to *Buddhism: The Path to Enlightenment*. *Buddhism: Footprint of the Buddha—India* together with *Buddhism: Be Ye Lamps unto Yourselves* and *Vejen* would provide a stimulating and worthwhile introduction to Theravada Buddhism in Sri Lanka, Thailand, and Burma.

Buddhism in China
  25 minutes, color, 16mm, 1973
  Sale $400.00, Rental $40.00
  Narrator: Alexander Scourby
  Director: Wan-Go Weng
  Producer: China Institute in America
  Distributor: Pictura Film Distribution Corp.
  Also available from: UIowa, UKans, UMich, PennSt, BYU, UWash

   This film treats the history of Buddhism in China through the use of maps, art, Chinese characters, and cinematic images to dramatize a wealth of information covered. It opens with a brief account of the Buddha's life and doctrine, mentioning the Noble Truths and the three disciplines. Tracing the spread of Buddhism to Central Asia and then to China, it also sketches the Confucian/Taoist cultural background within China. Buddhism in China proper is described by focusing on a number of major historical figures and several successive dynasties, with some colorful footage of the Tun Huang, Yun Kang, and Lung Men caves with their massive sculpture and elaborate frescos. The flowering of Chinese Buddhism in the T'ang dynasty gives occasion to describe the four schools: Hua Yen and Tien T'ai, considered as "doctrinal" schools, and the Pure Land and Ch'an, grouped together as "practical" schools. An elegant sequence of waves, grains of sand, the Buddha image reflected in multiple mirrors, bronze statues, and flowers in employed to convey a sense of the inconceivable "all-in-all" universe of the metaphysical schools. The film closes on a discussion of the harmony of the "Three Teachings" (Confucian, Taoist, and Buddhist) and some speculations about the value of Buddhism for modern man together with a pleasant sequence of a sunrise.

   This is the only competent film survey of Buddhism in China and as such is recommended for use in survey courses on Buddhism in China, or for independent viewing. It is reliable for the most part in its information and while its use of cinematic cliches is a mixed blessing, its tasteful use of ancient artwork is worth noting. This film does not deal with contemporary Chinese Buddhism. It might well be supplemented by the slide set *Chinese Religions* which treats contemporary practices in Hong Kong and Taiwan.

Buddhism: Land of the Disappearing Buddha—Japan
   54 minutes, color, 16mm, 1977
   Sale $750.00, Rental $100.00
   ¾" video cassette, Sale $200.00. ½" video cassette, Sale $150.00
   Narrator: Ronald Eyre
   Producer: Peter Montagnon for BBC
   Series: The Long Search
   Distributor: Time Life Video, Inc. (also available in videocassette)
   Also available from: UMich

   Focusing on the theme "Who or what is Buddha?," this film in The Long Search series looks at Japanese Buddhism by juxtaposing Zen and Pure Land Buddhism, as well as by brief excursions into Soka Gakkai and the Zen-related arts of swordsmanship, tea ceremony, calligraphy, and archery. Through interviews with both professional and lay religious practitioners, and through accompanying narration our disarming and generally unobstructive guide, Ronald Eyre, takes us from a "Zen restaurant" in Tokyo to a Zen master in Kobe, with stops along the way to search out other forms of Buddhism. During his treatment of the "Buddhism of self-reliance" (Zen), and what he calls the "Buddhism for learners" (Pure Land, Soka Gakkai), Eyre suggests that in Japan the Buddha "disappears" and the focus shifts instead to the realization of one's own true nature.

While the title of this film may be both awkward and misleading as a label for Japanese Buddhism generally and for Pure Land Buddhism specifically, and while a first viewing might be more confusing than clarifying, on balance the film is a good introduction for the beginning student to the thought and practice of selected Buddhist groups in contemporary Japan—both as expressed by representatives of the normative traditions and by the laity. The film tends to equate Buddhism with Zen—both explicitly in the opening sequences and implicitly in the idea of disappearing Buddhas—but this is partially corrected in the instructive coverage of Pure Land Buddhism. Similarly, the opening equation of Zen with restaurants and swords is corrected by the effective sequences on Zen life near the end of the film.

With the help of an introduction to the structure and intent of this film prior to viewing, this film could be useful both in and out of the classroom as a relatively careful, thoughtful, and introductory presentation of key contemporary forms of Japenese Buddhism. As such, it is better than other films such as *Japan: Land of the Kami,* or *The Gods of Japan.* Reading guides *(A Student's Guide to the Long Search,* prepared by Miami-Dade College, and *The Long Search* by Ninian Smart) have been prepared to accompany this series, but they do not accompany rental of the film.

Buddhism: The Path to Enlightenment
  30 minutes, color, 16mm, 1978
  Sale $350.00, Rental $35.00
  Producer: Elda Hartley
  Series: Films for a New Age
  Distributor: Hartley Film Foundation

This introduction to Theravada Buddhism focuses on religious life in Sri Lanka, although there are some scenes from Indian pilgrimage sites of Bodhgaya and Sarnath. The contents include a rehearsal of the life and a few basic teachings of the Buddha, archeological remains of the Buddhist civilization at Polonnaruwa, contemporary lay religious practices of offering oil-lamp lights and flowers before images of the Buddha, monastic activity—such as walking meditation, receiving food from laity, and circumambulating stupas—and about a five-minute coverage of the annual procession at Kandy to display the golden stupa-shaped container that is believed to hold a tooth of Buddha.

The photography is excellent, and while the coverage of Theravada religious life is selective, it shows some important aspects of Buddhist life in Sri Lanka. The narration is quite superficial and oversimplified; it reflects a clear bias toward the highly Western-educated Buddhist exponents of the tradition in its condescending comment on such lay expressions of Buddhism as offering flowers and incense at the Buddha's image. Some viewers might object to the sanctimonious tone of the narrator which makes the description seem less than sincere. For more effective introductions to Theravada Buddhism, see *Buddhism: Footprint of the Buddha—India* and *Buddhism: Be Ye Lamps unto Yourselves.*

Buddhist Art
  25 minutes, color, 16mm, n.d.
  Sale Japan only (contact producer, listed in Appendix of
  Distributors), Rental free
  Producer: Broadcast Programming Center of Japan
  Distributor: Japan Foundation

Using major examples of early Buddhist art and architecture in Japan as a basis, this film suggests by stylistic comparisons and historic origins the nature and scope of Buddhist iconography and temple architecture. The major examples are Buddha-figures at Horyuji, Hokaji, and Todaiji temples in Japan; early Buddha-images and Ajanta paintings in India; and selected comparable representations in China. Historically, the film suggests the development from an aniconic early Buddhism in India to the flowering of iconographic representation in India, China, and Japan.

Although this film is made in Japan and continually returns there as its point of reference, it is an attempt to see the larger context of Buddhist art. It is useful as such, but suffers from the incompleteness and oversimplification of all such surveys. While the film covers a good deal of the major types of iconographic representation in Mahayana, and offers suggestive comparisons at certain points, it is limited by an unsystematic presentation which continually moves back and forth between cultures, styles, and historical periods. Consequently, it may be somewhat confusing to the novice viewer, and might be best used where greater background or information can be presumed. In addition, the narration may be more appropriate to an art-history approach than a concern for these figures as Buddhist symbols.

The Buddhist World
  11 minutes, color, 16mm, 1963
  Sale $160.00, Rental $4.95

Consultant: Robert M. Perry
Distributor: Coronet Instructional Films
Also available from: UAriz, UCt, FlaSt, NoIll, SoIll, IndU, UIowa, UMe, BU, UMinn, KentSt, OklaSt, USoCar, BYU

The Buddhist World attempts a general survey of the history and teachings of Buddhism. The film focuses on a depiction of the early life of the Buddha, including an unconvincing reenactment by costumed actors of early events in Prince Siddhartha's life and a brief look at Indian historical sites. The film includes footage of Theravada rituals in Thailand and Zen gardens in Japan.

The film has numerous shortcomings. It suffers from excessive simplicity and generality, stereotypes, and cliches. Inaccuracies include the characterization of Tibetan Buddhist folk dances as war dances, and the assertion that Buddhist doctrine has changed very little over the centuries. It leaves the impression that Mahayana developed only outside of India, and that such Japanese cultural expressions as the tea ceremony are to be understood solely in terms of Zen.

Since other films (e.g., *Buddhism* in the Great Religions Series, or a combination of *The Buddha in South Asia, Buddhism in China* and *Buddhism: Land of the Disappearing Buddha—Japan)* perform this survey function more adequately, this film is not recommended for independent or classroom use.

Gautama the Buddha
78 minutes, b/w, 16mm, 1956
Sale in India only (To purchase, contact Government of India Films, Division listed in appendix of distributors). Rental free
Director: Rajbans Khanna
Producer: Bimal Roy
Distributor: Government of India

In two reels, this dated film recreates the life of the Buddha and portrays common village life in ancient India depicted in stone statues, relief carvings, paintings, and architectural remains. The first reel focuses on the details of bas-relief stone carvings. These are integrated with Indian music and a narration to create an experience of the market place, common entertainment, military activities, and lifestyles of holy men representative of the time when the Buddha lived. It uses the same technique to depict the Buddha's life from his immaculate conception through departure to practice austerities in the forest. The second reel depicts the Buddha's life from his meditation under the Bo-tree until his death, and the eventual dissemination of his message throughout Asia.

The use of images and bas-relief to portray the Buddha's life and ancient times is found in several films, such as *The Buddha* and *Land of Enlightenment,* but nowhere as effectively as here. The soundtrack of popular Indian music generally adds to the portrayal, although it sometimes lapses into sentimentality and is uneven in both volume and in clarity. The narration is more concerned with eliciting a positive spiritual response to Buddhist teaching than to enhance the viewers' understanding of the historical context in which the Buddha lived. The final minutes imply that the Buddha's message is the same throughout Asia—basically a mid-twentieth century, neo-Hindu perennial philosophy. Regrettably, the narration does not match the effectiveness of the imagery in relating the life of the Buddha.

The prints available for loan are generally in poor condition.

I Am a Monk
   30 minutes, color, 16mm, 1978
   Sale $325.00, Rental $35.00
   Producer: Elda Hartley
   Distributor: Hartley Film Foundations; also, CC Films

I Am a Monk explores the motivations, rewards, and life experiences of an American monk ("Michael") in Thailand. The frame for the film is provided by Michael's visit to his family in America and his return to Thailand, done with black-and-white photographs. Michael's decision to become a monk is depicted as a search for self-knowledge. The film focuses on meditation—a probing of all aspects of experience and a clearing away of the idea of self from the mind. Other aspects of Thai Buddhism and of Michael's experience are included. Alms rounds depict the relationship between monk and laity; Michael's student attendants illustrate social structure within the monastery and the veneration accorded the monk; the practice of herbal medicine by monks illustrates the social service rendered by the Sangha; and scenes from a meditation monastery in a rural area illustrate a diversity within monastic life. The ordination of Michael's friend, Jonathan, serves to encapsulate and symbolize Michael's own expectations and frustrations as a foreign monk in Thailand.

The film is useful in courses on Buddhism or for more general audiences. Although somewhat idealized, it is not too overstated. Michael tells his own story and in doing so provides a window not only to his own experience, but to the Theravada Buddhism of Thailand as well. This film might also be profitably used in conjunction with such films as *Tibetan Hertiage, Zen in Life, Buddhism: Be Ye Lamps unto Yourselves,* and other films on monastic training, or with films dealing with Buddhism in the West.

Mahayana Buddhism
  12 minutes, color, 16mm, 1969 (reissued periodically)
  Sale $180.00, Rental $20.00
  Producer: Lew Ayers
  Series: Altars of the World
  Distributor: Threshold Films

This is the second of a three-part series which also includes *Theravada Buddhism* and *Buddhism and Shintoism in Japan*. *Mahayana Buddhism* is a collage of scenes from Hong Kong and Taiwan with over-voice introductory explanations purporting to introduce Mahayana Buddhism. Strangely, half of the footage treats Confucianism and Taoism without an explanation of how they influenced Buddhism, and vice versa. Among its serious defects, this film perpetuates the misconception that Mahayana is a product solely of East Asia, it asserts that there were no Shakyamuni images in China, and it inadvertently mispronounces the name of the Buddha Amito-fo (boundless light) as "ami*tofu*" (boundless bean-curd).

Despite film footage on Chinese Buddhist nuns that may have historical interest for some viewers, this film cannot be recommended for class or independent use at any level. At the present time there is no general introductory film portraying Mahayana that can be recommended. Three effective films that show important segments of Mahayana Buddhism are *Buddhism in China, Tibetan Heritage,* and *Zen in Life.* A better survey of contemporary religion in Taiwan and Hong Kong can be found in the slide set *Chinese Religion.*

Meditation
  27 minutes, color, 16mm, 1968
  Sale none, Rental free
  Director/Producer: Paul Zils (Department of Information, Sri Lanka)
  Distributor: Tribune Films

Meditation is the story of a successful Sri Lanka doctor's decision to become a Buddhist monk as reenacted through a series of flashbacks. The film begins with the doctor going on a pilgrimage to Sri Pada, the site of Buddha's footprint in Sri Lanka, where he will prepare himself by meditation "for the most important event of my life"—ordination as a monk and "deliverance from the joys and sorrows of life." The film focuses on major episodes in the doctor's life: a childhood Vesak celebration (see *Vesak* review) in which the boy's beautiful paper lantern goes up in flames, his falling in love as a young medical student, his marriage, the death of his young bride in childbirth, and confrontation with the "cycle of birth and death, the daily spectacle of life's pain" as a doctor working among the poor. Each episode serves to dramatize the Buddha's teaching of life's impermanence (anicca) and pain (dukkha), the promptings of his quest for a higher goal through meditation and his decision to join the monastic order.

Despite its title, this film has very little to do with the actual practice of meditation. Rather, it is a dramatization of the Buddha's dharma (teaching), Unfortunately, the overall impression tends to be excessively stilted, with the consequence that instead of appearing as part of the fabric of life, the practice of Buddha's teaching seems staged and unreal. The colorful Vesak procession lacks the confused vitality often found at an authentic Vesak, and the contrived and orderly script gets in the way of the film's intent. The film's message will not be lost on general audiences, or those personally sympathetic to Buddhism, but it would appear to have problematical value for the classroom. For some audiences. *Awareness* might prove to be more engaging and *The Smile* is overall a more effective dramatization.

The Smile
20 minutes, color, 16mm, 1963
Out of print
Producer: Serge Bourguignon, Tamara Films
Also available from: FlaSt, USoFla, KentSt, UWise

This on-loation dramatization begins and ends with the ideal of Theravada Buddhism in Burma—wisdom and equanimity—embodied by the venerable monk Narada, who lives in a Rangoon monastery. Within this framework, the film depicts Burmese Buddhism through the experience of a young novice who is Narada's attendant. Through his eyes we see the morning food rounds (pindapata) in Rangoon, a long walk through Rangoon's surrounding countryside to an outlying monastery, and the famous Shwe Dagon Pagoda in the capital city.

The episodes along the way to the country monastery make up the bulk of the film. Together with the young boy we watch and touch a water buffalo in a field, wonder at a leaf worm's handiwork, smile at Burmese boxers, feel embarrassed by lovely girls bathing at a well, are delighted by the gift of an old cheroot-smoking lady, and are entertained by a puppet show. Finally, back in Rangoon, through the novice's attentive demeanor and actions, we offer respects to the venerable Narada and in doing so pay regard again to the ideals of Burmese Theravada Buddhism.

The Smile deserves the high acclaim it has received as a winsomely delightful cinematic experience. The sequence to the country monastery may seem overly drawn out for some viewers and its meaning somewhat ambiguous. The experiences of the young boy are engagingly developed, but does it really make a difference that he happens to be a novice monk? But then, this may well be precisely the question which the film is asking. What is the nameless truth of the religious life—the "smile" of the novice as he engages the world, or the monastic ideal as embodied by the venerable Narada?

Vejen brings out more varied aspects of institutional Buddhism in Burma and neither film is as encompassing an introduction to Theravada Buddhism in Southeast Asia as *Buddhism: Footprint of the Buddha*—India filmed in (Sri Lanka) or *Buddhism: Be Ye Lamps unto Yourselves* (Thailand).

Theravada Buddhism
  17 minutes, color, 16mm, 1966, reissued 1975
  Sale $225.00, Rental $23.00
  Narrator/Producer: Lew Ayers
  Series: Alters of the World
  Distributor: Threshold Films

Theravada Buddhism is the first of a three-part series on Buddhism. It is organized around four basic segments: the life of the Buddha, his teachings, the monastic community, and various Theravada practices. The Buddha's life is portrayed both through a brief look at historical sites associated with his career, and an ordination ceremony enacting the initiation of his mission. The film characterizes Theravada as a monastic faith, and as the national religion of several Southeast Asian countries. The doctrinal description includes mention of the metaphysics of karma, the Four Noble Truths, the Eightfold Noble Path, and Nirvana. The monastic community portion focuses on ordination and discipline among Theravada practices, including meditation, alms-giving, and worship.

This broad survey suffers from oversimplification, and a lack of cultural context. The film's inaccuracies include the claim that Theravada monks are always vegetarians. The doctrinal narration is inappropriately accompanied by footage of a Burmese ear-piercing ceremony. The brief and unhelpful study guide which accompanies the film makes misleading comparisons between Theravada and Mahayana.

Despite its wide distribution and ready availability this film is of doubtful value as a general introduction to Theravada Buddhism either for general or instructional use. *Buddhism: Footprint of the Buddha—India* and *Buddhism: Be Ye Lamps unto Yourselves* are superior films.

Vejen
  22 minutes, color, 16mm, 1971
  Sale $275.00, Rental $10.55

Director: Per Holst
Producer: Elsebet Kjolbye
Distributor: Carousel Films, Inc.
Also available from: UMich, KentSt

Vejen presents the ideals of Burmese Theravada Buddhism by focusing on the experience of a young boy in his capacity as an attendant to a monk, culminating in his ordination as a novice (shinbyu). The film moves from general scenes, particularly ritual activities at the Shwe Dagon pagoda in Rangoon, to the boy and his friends being instructed by the monk, to alms rounds (pindapata), and finally to the boy's ordination. The film's closing sequence provides a symbolically rich reenactment of the Buddha's going forth, a fitting conclusion to the visual episodes and narrative presentation of essential Buddhist teachings (e.g., karma) and ideals (e.g., Nirvana).

Vejen is a sensitively made and aesthetically effective interpretation of Theravada Buddhism. It conveys simplicity and directness without sacrificing the essential humanity or rich variety of Burmese Buddhism. The film also succeeds in integrating the polarity of levity and sobriety so characteristic of Southeast Asian Buddhism. This film is highly recommended for use in courses on Buddhism, particularly in its Southeast Asian, Theravada form. Valuable as a visual experience in and of itself, it can be used effectively as the basis of classroom discussion. Other films focusing on the monastic experience of a monk or novice include: *The Smile* (Burma), *I Am a Monk* (Thailand), *Zen Training of a Young Monk* (Japan), and *Tibetan Heritage* (Himalaya).

Zen In Life
25 minutes, color, 16mm, 1967
Sale Japan only, (Inquire, Orient Films Association, Tokyo, Japan)
Rental: $27.00
Producer: Nihon Film Center
Distributor: University of California—Berkeley

By focusing on the monasteries of Eiheiji and Sojiji, this beautiful film clearly depicts Zen discipline in traditional Soto Zen temples, and shows the effort to relate Zen teaching and practice to the contemporary layperson. Following one day's routine from the rising bell at 3 A.M. to the bedtime gong at 9 P.M. the first part of the film provides dramatic views of the interior of Eiheiji as well as views of the monks chanting in meditation, and at regular manual labor. The second half of the film focuses on the extension of Zen into everyday community life by showing the monks chanting services for laity; the education of young women; and the establishment by the Soto sect of a day-care service, an orphanage, a general hospital, and Komazawa University.

Visually, this is one of the best presentations of traditional Zen monastic life available on film. Despite occasional misleading comments, such as the interpretation of zazen (meditation) as "void of earthly ideas," most of the narrative is helpful. Unsophisticated comments, which sometimes seem to be more casual reporting than explanation, do not prevent this film from being a very useful aid in learning about Soto Zen practice. This film complements *Zen in Ryoko-In* by emphasizing the monastic aspect of Zen life. It can be used effectively to compare Zen training with that of Tibetan Buddhists, as seen in *A Prophecy*, and with that of Thai Buddhists, as seen in *Buddhism: Be Ye Lamps unto Yourselves*. This film might well be supplemented by use of the recording *The Way of Eheiji* with its accompanying notes on daily liturgy in the temple.

Zen in Ryoko-In
  71 minutes, color, 16mm, 1971
  Sale $595.00, Rental $55.00
  Director/Producer: Ruth Stephan
  Distributor: Ruth Stephan Films
  Also available from: UIll, SyrU

This beautiful film takes a close look at the daily routine of a small Zen temple within the larger Daitokuji complex in Kyoto, and at ceremonies and rituals related to the restoration and re-dedication of the main hall of that temple. In the process, it shows the functioning of a married priesthood, and how Zen relates to the lay and larger community in the comtemporary world. More specifically, the film is notable for its depiction of the important relation of Zen to the arts and aesthetic environment, family life in a Zen temple, the daily routine of a working temple, the rarely done "ceremony for the raising of the main timber" (jotoshiki), the ceremonies of completion and celebration when the restoration is finished, and the degree to which Shinto could participate in the ritual and symbolism at a Buddhist temple.

The presence of two individuals in this film is also worthy of mention. Ruth Stephan, an American poetess and producer of the film, appears for the most part unobtrusively but usefully with her poetry and her narrative description/interpretation. The temple's abbot, Nanrei Kobori, also appears significantly—both visually and by virtue of extremely insightful comments. While Ms. Stephan's presence might detract at points, both these people give the film (and Zen) an added charm and human quality unfortunately absent in most other films about Zen.

Some may feel this film to be unnecessarily long especially with its rather extended sequences in the second reel focusing on the ceremonies mentioned above. For those not interested in the latter, the first reel alone would be quite sufficient as a view of this exquisite temple and its life. This film nicely complements a treatment on Zen monastic training such as *Zen In Life* by its focus on temple life in Zen.

Slides

Buddha and His Teachings
25 slides, color, 1969
Sale $21.95 25-page text
Preparer: Rev. Shinjun J. Erwitt
Distributor: Scholarly Publications (formerly Sheikh Productions)

This set of 25 slides and accompanying texts attempts to show the life and teaching of the Buddha and the history and variety of Buddhism in Asia. Needless to say, it fails in this impossible task.

Buddhism
170 slides, color, n.d.
Sale $200.00, Rental $20.00
Producer: Kenneth W. Morgan
Distributor: Visual Education Service, Yale Divinity School
Accompanied by a 37 page booklet.

This collection of 170 colored slides shows Buddhist temples, pagodas, pilgrimage sites, and images from eight Asian countries. They are arranged by country. The first 21 show pilgrimage sites and iconographic art in India, primarily of Sarnath and Sanchi. The next four sections of about 20 slides each portray archeological sites and contemporary places of interest in Sri Lanka, Burma, Thailand, and Cambodia. Eleven slides on Chinese Buddhism were taken in Hong Kong and Rangoon; and 7 show Tibetan Buddhism as found in India. Forty-five slides of Japanese Buddhism depict a variety of temples, shrines, and images from different schools, although 17 of them show temples, meditating novices, and painted screens and scrolls found in Zen. A thirty-seven-page mimeographed booklet of notes on each slide accompanies the set.

This set includes many of the most renowned Buddhist places of interest in Asia, although it does not include pictures of Borobudur in Indonesia nor the cave Temples in China. It permits a glimpse of several important historical sites of Buddhism, and allows an introductory comparison of differences in monastic attire, temple architecture, and style of images in Buddhist countries. It does not provide views of major Buddhist festivals, and only a few of religious practice. In general, the quality of the photography is good, and the notes are useful.

The Buddhist Tradition: Buddhism in Burma
  80 frames, color, 1978
  Sale $20.00
  Producer: Argus
  Series: Religion in Human Culture
  Distributor: Argus Communications

This series of eighty slides focuses on institutional Buddhism in Burma. Some scenes from Thailand and Sri Lanka are included to accommodate the narration which is provided by a filmstrip guide and a cassette tape designed for either automatic or manual filmstrip equipment. The majority of the scenes relate to both lay and monastic religious practice. It begins with a visual impression of the significance of Buddhism to Burma, and continues to a depiction of the nature and goals of the monastic life, to the role of nuns, the relationships between monks and lay persons, and then to a novitiate ordination (shin-byu). The series then moves to popular Buddhism, concentrating first on the pagoda and various lay rites and activities performed there, and then on to the nat spirit cult and its relationship to Buddhism.

Overall, the explanation is adequately informative with only occasional misleading statements due to the level of generality of the presentation. The guide includes helpful interpretative comments as well as discussion questions and follow-up activities. The filmstrip is usefully supplemented by the volume on Buddhism in the Argus Major World Religion series. It is appropriate for high school, introductory college level, and adult general education purposes.

The Buddhist Tradition: Buddhism In Japan
  76 slides, color, 1978
  Sale $20.00
  Series: Religion in Human Culture
  Producer: World Religions Curriculum Development Center
  Distributor: Argus Communications

This series of 76 photographs introduces the student to Japanese religion, particularly Mahayana Buddhism in Japan. It begins by contrasting modern, industrialized Japan and traditional Japanese religion or Shintoism (slides 4–14). It then moves to Japanese Buddhism with attention to historical origins and founders, some of the major teachings of Mahayana Buddhism, the synthesis between Buddhism. Shinto, and Confucianism, and sectarian developments in the medieval period (slides 15–53). The final portion of the filmstrip (slides 53–76) includes various aspects of both popular and elite religious practice focusing on Zen. Mention is also made of the lay dominated New Religions which have arisen since the late nineteenth century.

This filmstrip provides a general orientation to the variety within Japanese religion, the historical development and teachings of Mahayana Buddhism in Japan, and the contributions of Buddhism to Japanese culture. The guide includes helpful interpretative comments as well as discussion questions and follow-up activities. The volume on Buddhism in the Argus Major World Religion series would supplement this filmstrip. The filmstrip is appropriate for high school and adult educational purposes.

Evolution of the Buddha Image
  74 slides, color, 1963
  Out of Print
  Producer: The Asia Society

This set of 74 slides was prepared from an exhibiton at Asia House in New York in 1963. The slides cover India (5-26), Nepal and Tibet (27-31), Southeast Asia (32-39), China (40-55), and Japan and Korea (56-74). Although images of stone, bronze, and wood predominate, paintings are included in the Nepal and Tibet, China, and Japan and Korea segments. The catalogue (*Evolution of the Buddha Image*, 1963), prepared by Benjamin Rowland, includes a descriptive/interpretative thirty-page introduction, and a technical description and explanation of each slide.

Although the quality of some slides is faded, the set remains one of the most effective tools for presenting the development of the Buddha image in Buddhist Asia, and might be used in conjunction with more focused visual studies in films such as *The Glory That Remains, The Buddha: Temple Complex at Borobudur*, or *Thai Images of the Buddha*.

History of the Oriental Arts
  300 slides (15 sections of 20 slides each), color
  Sale $30.00 per section
  Producer: Bijuts Shoppon Sa
  Distributor: Prothman Associates

Of interest to teachers of Buddhism are sections B and C on Chinese art from Wei through T'ang Dynasties, set G on Korean and Central Asian art, sets I and J on Indian art, and set L on Ceylon, Indonesian, and Cambodian art. The slides in these sets are arranged in the context of providing a basic survey course on Oriental art. While they do not intend to illustrate Buddhism per se, they do provide a good contextual background for the art of the different cultures where Buddhism flourished, and they do include numerous attractive and important examples of Buddhist art and architecture. The slides are well photographed and reproduced, and identified by subject, provenence, and date.

Marks and Mudras of the Buddha
  50 slides, color, n.d.
  Sale $20.00, Rental none
  Producer: Frank and Phyllis Smarto
  Distributor: New York University Asian Studies Curriculum Center

This slide set is an intelligently conceived teaching tool giving a solid introduction to the iconography of the Buddha. Major iconographic marks of the Buddha including ushnisha, hair, fingers, toes, posture, wheel marks, and so forth, are each clearly shown and explained. The slides show a broad selection of styles and include examples of Buddhist Art from India, Southeast Asia, China, and Japan. While the commentary and selection are useful to show the subject, it must be stated the visual quality of the slides varies from poor to acceptable.

Monk's Ordination Ceremony
  50 slides, color
  Sale $20.00, Rental none
  Producer: Emma Jane Reilly
  Distributor: New York Curriculum Center University Asian Studies

This set presents a pedagogically useful overview of ordination in the social context of Thailand. The first fifteen slides give general background on when and why a Thai man enters the monastic community (usually for three months). The remaining slides focus on the steps of the ritual and the general festivity accompanying this ceremony. The steps of ordination shown include initial training, tonsure, novitiates' ordination, and higher ordination (unpasampada). The guide provides brief descriptions of each slide and gives a good sense of what might be seen on the occasion of ordination. However, the guide does not go deeply enough into either social or philosophical issues, and the slides are not of professional quality.

The World's Great Religions—Buddhism
  2 filmstrips with cassettes (105 frames), 1973
  Sale $50.00
  Teachers Guide and Student Materials by David Whalen
  Distributor: Time Life Video, Inc.
  Series: The World's Great Religions

This set is an updated version of an earlier Time Life slide set on world religions. It includes many splendid visuals and some tragic ones such as a monk's self immolation in Vietnam. The narrative aims to provide a very general overview of Buddhism, but it has some serious flaws. Its attempts to differentiate among Theravada, Mahayana, and Tantric Buddhism are very misleading, and many words are mispronounced. The narrative usually does not identify or explain what is being shown on the filmstrip. Instead, it relies on the visuals for a panorama of monks, temples, paintings, and scenic views from Asia, only loosely related to the lecture. The filmstrip and cassette come with a reprint of *Life* magazine articles from 1955 and 1967, as well as with ditto sheets of questions for students.

Recordings

Religious Music of Asia
  Recorded by Charles A. Kennedy. Notes by Charles A. Kennedy
  Distributor: Folkways Records (FE 4481)

Band eight on side one is an unidentified liturgy performed by Nepalese Buddhist monks. The notes comment on the strangeness of the sound and the elementary instruments. Side two, band one is an unidentified excerpt of a Chinese Buddhist priest chanting during the celebration of Buddha's birthday. Band two is Chinese Buddhist nuns chanting a service commissioned by visitors to a temple. Band three is a modernized band in a parade celebrating visala. Band four is a Zen morning service, half in English. Band five is chanting of the revered Zen monk Hakuin's "Hymn to Meditation (Dhyana)." The final Buddhist piece is a Zen drum call.

The notes are simplistic and somewhat patronizing in tone. Kennedy wrongly stresses the similarity of all Buddhist music stating, "A common source of cantillation influences all the variations heard in Buddhist services from India to Japan: there is the same hypnotic drone, the flagrant disregard of pitch and the absence of instrumental accompaniment."

CHAPTER 2

South Asia

Films

The Buddha in South Asia*
Buddhism: Footprint of the Buddha—India*
Buddhism: The Path to Enlightenment*
Cave Temples of India—Buddhist
Guatama the Buddha*
The Glory That Remains (formerly Sermons in Stone)
Immortal Stupa
In the Steps of the Buddha
Land of Enlightenment
Meditation*
Nagarjunakonda
Nalanda
Pearl of the East
Sermons in Stone (see under The Glory That Remains)
Song of Ceylon
Vesak

Slides

Ajanta: Architecture, Sculpture, and Painting (slides)
Ceylon—Paintings from Temple, Shrine and Rock
Early Buddhist Art of Stupas The Great Stupa at Sanchi
India: Paintings from Ajanta Caves
Sanchi

*Reviewed in Section I: General and Historical Introductions.

Films

Cave Temples of India—Buddhist
  9 minutes, b/w, 16mm, 1961
  Sale: India only (Write to the Government of India Films Division.
  See appendix of distributors), Rental free
  Director: Jagat Murari
  Producer: M. Bhavnani
  Distributor: Government of India

Following a brief statement about the Buddha and King Ashoka, this film presents a survey of the famous cave (lena) temples of the Western Ghat region of India which flourished from the first through the eighth centuries A.D.

Beginning with the earliest rock sculpture in India at Bhagh (mid-first century A.D.) the film moves briefly to Kanari (second to sixth century A.D.) before showing the Ajanta caves. The Ajanta sequence includes a presentation of the sloping caitya pillars of cave 10; the outstanding frescoes of bodhisattvas, heavenly beings, demons, and ruling elites in caves 1 and 17; the elaborate vihara (assembly hall) of cave 1; and the ornate mid-sixth century facade of cave 19. A brief look at the two Buddhist caves at Ellora is included in this sequence.

The film provides a useful, although brief, overview of the development of the Buddhist cave temple/monastery sculpture in India. Unfortunately, no attempt is made to relate this Buddhist art and architectural development to historical and ideational changes in Indian Buddhism.

This film is appropriate for classes in Asian art history, and would be useful for the study of Buddhism when supplemented by materials on the historical and philosophical evolution of Indian Buddhism. Note should be made of excellent slide sets on Ajanta and other Indian cave temples. The print of the film was in poor condition.

The Glory that Remains (formerly Sermons in Stone)
  30 minutes, color, 16mm, 1969
  Discontinued
  Writer: Robert Erskine
  Producer: Adrian Malone for BBC-TV
  Series: Sermons in Stone
  Distributor: Time Life Video, Inc. (discontinued, inquire BBC, London)
  Also available from: PennSt

This film appreciatively shows and explains the pillars of King Ashoka, the stupas, railings and gateways of Sanchi, and various images of Gautama the Buddha. Specifically, it shows several pillars, close-up views of the lion capital at Sarnath, Kalinga rock inscriptions and examples of rock crystal containers used to hold relics in stupas. The scenes from Sanchi include an overview of the site, views of the main stupas and extensive examination of the bas-relief figures on gateways and railings. These close-ups portray expressions of everyday life, scenes from the life of the Buddha, and popular figures (e.g., a yakshi holding to a tree limb). The Sanchi expressions of aniconic representations of the Buddha—as images of the Bo-tree, wheel or stupa—are distinguished from later human images of Gautama the Buddha.

By effectively showing the workmanship and artistic quality of the pillars and carvings, this film makes it easy to appreciate the great artistry of Buddhist sculpture. The Buddha's teaching, which is only briefly described, is regarded primarily as an ethic of compassion. At several points, the narrator—whose speech mannerisms may prove difficult for some American viewers—compares Buddhist art and thought with Christian art and thought. These comparisons are sometimes oversimplified to the point of distorting the message of the Buddha in its historical context. The cinematography is effective. This film is recommended for use at an introductory level of study. It is superior to *Immortal Stupa*, which also shows details of the stupa at Sanchi.

Immortal Stupa
  14 minutes, b/w, 16mm, 1961
  Sale India only, (To purchase, contact Government of India Films
  Division listed in appendix of distributors). Rental free
  Producer: Bhimal Roy
  Distributor: Government of India

This black-and-white film documents Sanchi, one of the oldest Buddhist monuments in the world. More particularly, it focuses on the bas-reliefs of the four gateways at the cardinal directions around the stupa itself, with specific discussion of their iconographic detail: (1) South Gateway—Ashoka's distress at the withering of the Bo-tree; the war over the Buddha relics;(2) East Gate—the Yaksha pillars, the temple at Bodhgaya, the miracle of the Buddha's walking on the water, homage paid to the Buddha by kings as well as animals, the great renunciations;(3) North Gate—ascent of the Buddha to preach to his mother in the Tavatimsa Heaven, the temptation of the Buddha, the Vessantara Jataka;(4) West Gate—different modes of earthly existence, the first discourse at Sarnath.

Primarily of art-historical interest, this film neglects the significance of Sanchi as a pilgrimage center and does not discuss the importance of the bas-reliefs for an understanding of popular Buddhism. The film similarly fails to discuss the symbolism of the stupa and the reasons for early Buddhism's aniconic attitude toward the Buddha. Despite its rather faded quality, this film could be of educational value for a general audience or courses on Buddhism when used by a resourceful instructor with sufficient competence in Indian Buddhism. For a better treatment of the same subject, see *The Glory That Remains.*

In the Steps of the Buddha
19 minutes, color, 16mm, n.d.
Sale none, Rental free
Producer and Director: P. Hettarachi for Department of Information, Sri Lanka
Distributor: Tribune Films

This film presents selected episodes in the life of the Buddha and the spread of his teachings in Sri Lanka as found in the *Dipavamsa* chronicle and depicted primarily in the justly famous modern mural paintings at Kelaniya outside of Colombo, Sri Lanka. In particular, it focuses on the three visits of the Buddha to the island as recorded in the *Dipavamsa*: the conversion of the aboriginals and the enshrinment of Buddha relics; bringing peace to warring factions through his teaching of non-attachment; his visit to Sumanakuta (Adam's Peak) and Kelaniya, two important pilgrimage sites. In addition to the paintings, scenes from Anuradhapura and Polonnaruwa are included, as well as footage of a pilgrimage up Sumanakuta.

This film will have a limited appeal to a general audience. For classroom use it will require extensive explanation. However, if used in conjunction with a discussion of the nature of chronicle materials in Theravada Buddhism and their relationship with popular piety, it would be of instructional value. Through the device of pilgrimage to sacred places in Bihar state in India, *Land of Enlightenment* more effectively shows the historical development of Buddhism.

Land of Enlightenment
12 minutes, b/w, 16mm, 1953
Sale: India only (To purchase, contact Government of India Films Division listed in the appendix of distributors). Rental free
Director: Mohan Wadhwani
Producer: M. Bhavanani
Distributor: Government of India

Through the device of a pilgrimage to sacred places and historical sites, this film shows some of the key locations in the sacred geography of Bihar in India. The Buddhist holy places are organized around the life of Buddha, with emphasis on Sarnath and Bodhgaya. Also included is some footage on the ruins of the Buddhist monastic university at Nalanda, and the artifacts housed in the Patna Museum. Besides Buddhist points of interest, the film shows a Sikh temple and Hindu holy places.

Using a travelogue format which might be distracting for some viewers, this black-and-white film has the limitations of a dated documentary style. It is perhaps most useful for viewers already familiar with Indian religious sites. Some viewers will find the Hindi pronunciation of place names and terms unfamiliar. At times, narration tends to be confusing because it does not discriminate between various Indian religious traditions, and it emphasizes selected general concepts of Indian spiritual life. For a color film that shows early Buddhist imagery and sacred sites in India and which is of better overall quality see *The Glory That Remains*.

Nagarjunakonda
    17 minutes, b/w, 16mm, 1958
    Sale India only (To purchase, contact Government of India Films Division listed in the appendix of distributors). Rental free
    Director: S. N. S. Sastry
    Producer: Ezra Mir
    Distributors: Government of India

This film seeks to depict the glorious past of a historical Buddhist site on the banks of the Krishna River in Southern India. Scenes of ancient foundations and pillars of halls, chapels, and monastic cells are combined with closeup shots of stone-reliefs which tell the life of the Buddha and the activities of celestial bodhisattvas. A royal sacrificial and purification site used by Hindu kings is described. The size of chapels, and of a stadium where thousands could meet for rituals of reverence and dedication to the teaching of the Buddha, as well as numerous monastery sites in the valley area, indicate the importance of Nagarjunakonda during the third and fourth centuries A.D.

The background consists of popular Indian music reminiscent of contemporary commercial Indian films. The narration of the Buddha's life is poorly integrated with the footage of archeological remains. While this film portrays an important historical site, viewers should be cautioned about misleading general statements regarding Buddhist history and teaching, and about the use of Western religious terminology in describing Buddhist experience.

Nalanda
    10 minutes, b/w, 16mm, 1962
    Sale India only (To purchase, contact Government of India Films
    Division listed in appendix of distributors). Rental free
    Director: Arun Chaudhuri
    Narrator: Zul Vellani
    Producer: K.L. Khandpur for Films Division of India
    Distributor: Government of India

This is a reverent portrayal of the center of secular and spiritual
learning (mahavihara) at Nalanda in northern India. Through an
overview of the ruins and partial reconstruction of this ancient
university, close-up footge of remnant foundations, archways, drain-
age system, and Buddha images, with a narration suggesting the
activities of former monks who lived there, this film reveals the
immensity and complexity of this center of Mahayana Buddhism
during the sixth century A.D. The film stresses the tolerance shown
among various Buddhist schools as well as the breadth of study found
there, including training in Hindu materials, logic, and ceramic
technology. The underlying message is the glorious past of ancient
India in which Nalanda participated by spreading a message "in
keeping with all that is good in man."

This black-and-white documentary effectively portrays an important Indian historical site, but the dated style will be less attractive to an
introductory class than to viewers well versed in the history of the
Buddhist religious tradition. Some students may have difficulty in
understanding the Indian-accented English narration. Some generalizations about Mahayana Buddhism and the decline of Buddhism in
India would be misleading without further explanation. Brief scenes
of Nalanda are also shown in *Land of Enlightenment*.

Pearl of the East
    28 minutes, color, 16mm, n.d., out of print
    Narrator: Lowell Thomas
    Series: World of Lowell Thomas
    Producer: Duman Griffin-Beale for Odessy Productions and BBC-
    TV
    Distributor: Peter M. Robeck and Co.

Using a travelogue format, this film focuses on various colorful and
dramatic aspects of life in Sri Lanka. Overall, it emphasizes how
aspects of Buddhism, Hinduism, and folk animistic practices merge in
the Sri Lankan social experience. It shows scenes of Pambulk temples;
the torch and light procession of the Buddha's tooth in Kandy; part of

Buddhist ordination ceremony; Kataragama; ecstatic Hindu devotees with skewers through their cheeks or suspended in mid-air by large hooks, or pilgrims rolling their bodies many miles to a shrine; and the frenzied dancing of a group of devotees seeking to sure a patient possessed by spirits.

The overall impact of the film is a collage of tourist curiosities. Little information is given to interpret what is seen and oversimplifications abound. Offerings to the Buddha are called "food for the gods" and it is also claimed that "in Ceylon elephants are considered holy." Despite several important and dramatic scenes depicting Sri Lanka, this film has limited usefulness in giving an understanding of Theravada Buddhism or the interaction of Buddhism and society. For a better introduction to Sinhalese Buddhism, see *Buddhism: Footprint of the Buddha—India*. Also the film *Vesak* is useful to show the important Vesak festival and the interaction between monastic Buddhism and popular religious life.

Song of Ceylon
  33 minutes, b/w, 16mm, 1935, out of print
  Director: Basil Wright
  Producer: John Grierson for Denning Films
  Also available from: UCB, IndU, UMich, SyrU, UWash

Song of Ceylon won a first prize at the Brussels Film Festival in 1935 and is considered an early ethnographic classis. The film is divided into four segments: Buddha, Virgin Island, Voices of Commerce, and The Apparel of a God. The first treats Buddhism, focusing largely on a pilgrimage to Sri Pada or Adam's Peak with occasional clips from Polonnaruwa. The point is made that Buddhism displaced an older shamanistic/animistic religion represented by some shots of devil dancers. The second segment deals with selected aspects of traditional life and culture, including fishing, rice production, pottery manufacture, lumbering, and the training of Kandian dancers. The third segment puts agriculture of Ceylon (Sri Landa) into the international-export context determined by its status as part of the British Commonwealth. The final portion of the film returns us to Buddhism via worship of the Buddha, represented first by a modest offering made before the reclining Buddha image at Polannaruwa and then by Kandian dancers.

This black-and-white film may be of historical interest as an ethnographic document but is not recommended for the study of Buddhism. See *Buddhism: Footprint of the Buddha—India* for a more adequate treatment of Buddhism in Sri Lanka.

Vesak
   18 minutes, color, 16mm, 1975
   Sale $250.00, Rental $25.00
   Director/Producer: Yvonne Hanneman
   Distributor: Focus International, Inc.

Vesak is a cultural film on the festival of Vesak in Sri Lanka, celebrating the birth, enlightenment, and final Nirvana of the Buddha —all traditionally believed to have occurred on the same date. The film opens with a general description of Sri Lanka (Ceylon) and its people, with emphasis on the Sinhalese populace, and then proceeds to unfold the Vesak celebration in two segments: preparations for the festival and the celebration itself. Preparation focuses on the construction of elaborate lanterns and bilboards celebrating stories about previous existences of the Buddha (Jataka tales). The Vesak celebration itself begins with lay processions to Buddhist temples and the offering of flowers, incense and candles to the Lord Buddha. For some of the participants, this full moon day (poya) in May will be spent at the temple; for others it is an occasion for sightseeing and recreation.

This film revealingly depicts popular religion in Sri Lanka and the interaction between monastic and lay Buddhism. The cinematography and narration focus on such popular practices as the making of paper lanterns and Buddha offerings. If more attention had been paid to the normative significance of the event and its attendant ritual practices, the film would have been even more useful for courses in Buddhism. Nevertheless, *Vesak* is recommended for both independent and classroom use. *Buddhism: Footprint of the Buddha—India* offers a better introduction to Buddhism in Sri Lanka, and *Pearl of the East* provides broader cultural background. For a film focusing on a popular Buddhist festival in Japan, see *Jizo Children's Festival*.

Slides

Ajanta: Architecture, Sculpture, and Painting
   100 slides, color, n.d.
   Sale $100.00
   Distributor: American Committee on South Asian Art

This set shows the Ajanta caves from an art-historical perspective. Excellent photography but minimum identifications characterize this and the other ACSAA sets. Slides show views of the overall site of the caves in a secluded valley in Maharashtra, India. Details show sculpture and painting from caves #1, 2, 4, 6, 7, 9, 10, 12, 17, 19, 20, 21, 22, 23, 24, and 26, including appropriate views of the Buddha preaching, receiving the gift of sujata, and in parinirvana pose. Sculpture of the Jatakas and the temptation of the Buddha is not shown in sufficient detail to be comprehensible to the untrained eye.

Ceylon—Paintings From Temple; Shrine and Rock
   30 slides, color, n.d.
   Sale $26.00 Trilingual guide
   Producer: UNESCO
   Distributor: UNIPUB

This set attempts in thirty slides to span the whole history of painting in Sri Lanka from the fifth to the nineteenth century. Slides 1–10 are fifth century; Slides 11–14 are eighth century; Slides 15-21 are from the eleventh and twelth centuries.

The remainder are in eighteenth and nineteenth century "Kandyan" style. There is little attempt to relate these markedly different styles either with developments in Buddhism or with art history. Even though the art is entirely of Buddhist subjects and from Buddhist sites, this set is only marginally useful in the study of Buddhism. For example, the first ten slides are of the beautiful women attendants depicted in surviving frescoes from the Sigiri rock of the fifth century. The guide points out the similarities in both construction and artistic style of these frescoes and the frescoes of Ajanta. Many of the other slides are also of ancillary figures, including closeups of Hindu gods and their attendants from larger frescoes. Of the collection, only the modern Kandian-style paintings depict recognizable scenes from the life of the Buddha and Jataka tales.

Early Buddhist Art of the Stupas
   100 slides, color, n.d.
   Sale $100.00
   Distributor: Government of India

This set provides excellent visual perspective of the major sites of Barhut, Amaravati, Sanchi, Nagarjunikonda, and Bodhgaya. Sculptural detail is shown, including scenes from Jatakas and the life of the historical Buddha.

The Great Stupa At Sanchi
   40 slides, color, n.d.
   Sale $15.00 (21-page typescript guide)
   Producer: Elizabeth Sierzega
   Distributor: New York University Asian Studies Curriculum Center

These slides comprise a student's report on Sanchi, showing panoramic views, drawings, and maps from books and details of the monument. The guide is an unpretentious explanation of the religous significance of the site and the sculptures depicting episodes from the Buddha's life. While this set should be commended for its attention to religious concerns, the quality of the slides is not on a par with those sets designed by and for art historians (e.g., *Sanchi* and *Early Buddhist Art of the Stupas*).

India: Paintings From Ajanta Caves
   30 slides, color, n.d.
   Sale $26.00 (Trilingual guide)
   Producer: UNESCO
   Series: UNESCO Art Slides
   Distributor: UNIPUB

These slides provide details of some of the Buddhist paintings at Ajanta. The guide gives a brief historical background and discusses the place of these paintings in the development of Indian art styles and motifs. Of special interest for the teacher of religion is the section of the guide (pp.30-35) describing the themes of the paintings including details of the depiction of the Mahajanaka Jataka Tabe (slides 2-9), and the Visvantara Jataka (slides 18-20 and 23-25). The slides themselves are visually adequate, but not equal in clarity to those in the ACSAA collection.

Sanchi
   50 slides (accompanied by 5x8 index cards showing black and white views, with identifications and extensive notes)
   Producers: Walter M. Spink and Deborah Levine
   Photographs: Asian Art Archives (University of Michigan 1969)
   Distributor: Interbook

This slide set should be taken as a model of what can and should be done in preparing a slide lecture on a religious monument. The photographs are very high quality. Further, this set excels in the convenient format of the descriptive notes and the information they provide the viewer or lecturer.

Sanchi was an important center of Buddhism in India from at least the time of Ashoka (third century B.C.) through the sixth century A.D. The stupas, temples, and sculpture constitute a priceless historical record of changes in Buddhism, as well as a source of delightful visual information on Buddhist iconography, art, and architecture. The notes *explain* what the beautiful elephants, lotuses, and wheels stand for. They discuss changes in the monuments in terms of which emperors supported Buddhism, and why. They also discuss stylistic differences that would be noted by art historians but in a fashion that would be readily intelligible to a class in religion, and they dwell at length on sculptural depictions of the life of the Buddha and of

Ashoka, while quoting from traditional biographies. While the slides themselves have lost some of their color, they are still visually attractive and present well-photographed views arranged in an intelligent lecture. This set can be used as an introduction to the development of Buddhist art, as visual evidence of the transition from the Theravada to more metaphysical forms of Buddhism, to show depictions of the life of the Buddha, to discuss the importance of lay patronage for the development of Buddhism, or as a supplement to an overview of Indian Buddhism. In all of these situations, the notes and the slides provide a useful tool for classroom or individual study.

CHAPTER 3

Southeast Asia

Films

Angkor Wat: The Ancient City
Angkor: The Lost City
Borobudur: The Cosmic Mountain
The Buddha: Temple Complex a Borobudur
Buddhism: Be Ye Lamps unto Yourselves*
Burma, Buddhism and Neutralism
Chiang Mai, Northern Capital
I Am a Monk*
The Smile*
Temple of the Twenty Pagodas
Thai Images of the Buddha
Thailand
Thailand: Land of Smiles
Vejen*

Slides

L'Art Khmer
Buddhism in Southeast Asia and Ceylon
The Buddhist Tradition: Buddhism in Burma*
Monk's Ordination Ceremony*
The Story of the Buddha in Thai Murals

Recordings

The Music of Cambodia
The Music of Viet Nam—I
The Music of Viet Nam—II

*Reviewed in Section I: General and Historical Introductions

Angkor: The Lost City
  12 minutes, b/w, 16mm, 1961
  Sale none, Rental $3.40
  Producer: Roger Blair for National Film Board of Canada
  Distributor: The Pennsylvania State University
  Also available from: USoFla, UIll, OklaSt, UUtah, WashSt, UWisc

This film provides an overview of Angkor, one of the greatest archi-
tectual achievements in the world and a testimony to the grandeur
of the Khmer civilization from the ninth to the fifteenth century. The
film begins with an effective presentation of the rediscovery and
reconstruction of Angkor by the French, beginning in 1860. Referring
to Chinese chronicles and Khmer stone inscriptions, it gives an idea of
the historical development of the capital, Angkor Thom, and the
sacred sanctuary/cosmic mountain, Angkor Wat. The film includes a
discussion of the god-king concept so central to the symbolism of
Angkor by focusing on the justly famous Jayavarman VII (1181-1218),
the hydraulic engineering of the capital, the social and military history
as depicted in the elaborately detailed stone reliefs, and the eclecticism
of Khmer religion as represented by the images of Vishnu, Shiva, and
the Buddha.

Although the Buddhist significance of the monument is not made
apparent, *Angkor: The Lost City* succeeds in revealing one of the most
important historical monuments in Asia—including its genesis, what
it represents, how it was destroyed, and then rediscovered. Recommended for general audiences or for cultural background for courses
dealing with religion in Southeast Asia, the film might be used along
with books such as: Robert Heine-Geldern's *Concepts of State and
Kingship in SE Asia* (1956), or Hermann Kulke's *The Devraja Cult*
(1978). It is superior to the film *Angkor Wat: The Ancient City* (see
review).

Angkor Wat: The Ancient City
  15 minutes, color, 16mm, 1963
  Sale $155.00 Rental $15.00
  Producer: Fleetwood Films
  Distributor: Macmillan Films, Inc.
  Also available from: UIowa, BU

This film provides a travelogue overview of Angkor, the capital of
the Khmer Empire from the ninth to the end of the fourteenth century.
It begins with Angkor Wat, a "temple dedicated to Hindu Gods," and
includes shots of its four-mile moat, bas-reliefs, the Bayon temple
within the walls of Angkor Thom (the capital), and stone carvings of
battle scenes.

The narrator's reference to Angkor as Cambodia's "foremost tourist attraction" aptly characterizes the level of this film. Although some useful footage of Angkor Wat and Ankgor Thom is included, very little is provided about the Hindu-Buddhist sycretism of Khmer religion. The Bayon is not identified and its faces representing Jayavarman VII, the God-King (Buddha-raja and Deva-raja) are referred to as "stone masks." The film omits a discussion of the meaning of the reliefs or the symbolism of the monument, and moves from scene to scene to a musical accompaniment more appropriate to Latin America than Southeast Asia. It is recommended that *Angkor: The Lost City* be used instead.

Borobudur: The Cosmic Mountain
   40 minutes, color, 16mm, 1972
   Sale not in U.S.
   Director/Producer: Brian Brake
   Distributor: Zodiac Films, Hong Kong
   Also available from: UCB, UMich.

Borobudur has several facets: a cinemagraphic depiction and explanation of this ninth-century Buddhist monument, a presentation of traditional Indonesian cultural arts, and an appeal for support for the restoration of the Borobudur stupa. The film has five main segments which intertwine Borobudur with the past, present, and future of Indonesia: an introductory overview of Java, Borobudur, and Jogjakarta; a brief exploration of the structure and meaning of Borobudur; classical cultural arts of the court gamelan and dance, batik, and puppet theatre; the history of, and contemporary efforts toward, the restoration and preservation of the stupa; and an overview of the early history of Java culminating in the great Hindu and Buddhist monuments of the eighth and ninth centuries. The film closes with a Buddhist puja or worship conducted at Borobudur.

Although the film has some beautiful photography of Borobudur and Java, its segmentation prevents sufficient focus on the monument itself. Various interpretations of Borobudar—a mountain built to glorify ancestors; a stupa enshrining the Buddha, a three-dimensional mandala; a tower of the Budhist law; a cosmic mountain of the universe—are only mentioned. In spite of an occasional touristic visual technique, this film is useful for courses on the culture of Indonesia, and more generally the history and culture of Southeast Asia. For the film to be used effectively, however, it should be supplemented by readings and lectures on the monument (e.g., Henri Parmentier, Borobudur, or Paul Mus, *Barabudur*). Unlike *The Buddha: Temple Complex at Borobudur* which shows only bas-reliefs, this film presents the whole monument and the culture of which it is a part.

The Buddha: Temple Complex of Borobudur
  11 minutes, 16mm, Sepia, 1960
  Sale $175.00, Rental $15.00
  Director/Producer: Henre Dore
  Distributor: Film Images/Radim Films; also, University of Chicago Audio Visual Center

This film shows the life of the Buddha as depicted in sculpture at the great ninth-century Buddhist monument, Borobudur, on the island of Java, Indonesia. Pictures of selected bas-relief carvings at Borobudur are interspersed with narrative captions to depict some key scenes in the life of the Buddha up to his enlightenment. There is no narrative over-voice explanation, and the sound track is entirely of Indonesian gamelan music. There is no overall aerial view of the Borobudur temple complex. These limitations, in addition to the poor quality of the soundtrack and print, make this film of limited usefulness. For a more complete portrayal of Borobudur, see *Borobudur: The Cosmic Mountain.*

Burma, Buddhism and Neutralism
  55 minutes, b/w, 16mm, 1957
  Sale $150.00, Rental $10.70
  Narrator: Edward R. Murrow
  Director: Paul Nevin
  Distributor: University of Michigan

Narrated by Edward R. Murrow, this film depicts Burma in the 1950s. The film presents Buddhism as integral to Burma's national identity, Burma's neutralism under U Nu's 'Buddhist Socialism', and its anticommunist stance. Although some aspects of Burmese Buddhist practice are included, the film focuses on U Nu's interpretation of Buddhism and its significance for Burmese nationhood.

This film has little instructional utility for classes on traditional Buddhism in Southeast Asia. Its primary value lies in its presentation of the interfacing of Buddhism and politics in U Nu's Burma, and its reflection of 1950s popular American attitudes toward Burmese neutralism. Consequently, the film is of historic interest for those interested in Buddhism and nationalism in Southeast Asia. Sarkisyanz, *Buddhist Backgrounds of the Burmese Revolution* (see and Donald Smith, *Religion and Politics in Burma*, for interpretations of the topic.)

Chiang Mai, Northern Capital
  15 minutes, color, 16mm, 1971
  Sale $190.00, Rental $3.75

Director: Brian Hannant
Producer: John Morris and Thanom Soonaratna
Series: Our Asian Neighbors (Thailand)
Distributor: Australian Information Services (rental) Sterling Educational Films (sale)

This film is a presentation of selected aspects of traditional northern Thai culture. Although it includes segments on cock fighting and such traditional crafts as silver manufacture, lacquerware, and silk weaving, the bulk of the film treats two significant and photogenic festivals: the presentation of new robes to monks at the end of the rains retreat (thod kathin), and the festival of lights propitiating the goddess of waters and the ancestral spirits (loi krathong). The segment on the thod kathin includes a colorful procession, dancing, ceremonial sword fighting, and the presentation of gifts to the monks. The loi krathong sequence treats the rather commercialized Chiang Mai procession complete with beauty queens, the temple celebration at Wat Cedi Luang, and the floating of small banana leaves and more elaborate *krathongs* on the Mae Ping river. The small boys who swim out to swipe the coins from the krathongs contribute a light and authentic touch to this sequence.

This film is useful for general audiences or for presenting a cultural background for the study of Buddhism and culture in Southeast Asia. *Buddhism: Be Ye Lamps Unto Yourselves* provides more specific material on Buddhism in Thailand. See *Vesak* and *Jizo Children's Festival* for Buddhist festivals in Sri Lanka and Japan respectively.

Temple of the Twenty Pagodas
  22 minutes, color, 16mm, 1971
  Sale $255.00, Rental $5.00
  Director: Brian Haunant
  Producer: John Morris and Thanom Soonaratna
  Series: Our Asian Neighbors
  Distributor: Australian Information Services
  Also available from: UCB, NoIll

After a brief introduction, this film provides no narration as the camera follows monks and laity during a day's activities in a Theravada Buddhist temple-monastery (wat) outside of Lampang, northern Thailand. Monks are shown chanting in the temple, going into town to receive food, cleaning the temple precincts, studying, eating a noon meal, reading, and speaking to a lay audience. The camera moves outside of the monastery compound to farmers in nearby rice fields and follows school children playing inside the compound, thereby illustrating the fluid boundaries of the Thai wat. The variety of activities touched on brings out both traditional and changing monastic roles.

This film contains some beautiful scenes of Thai Buddhist temple architecture and images. It also shows some important monastic activities and the interaction between lay and monastic communities of Thai Buddhism. However, the lack of narration to explain such activities as the purchase of amulets or monks prostrating before the image of the Buddha limits the film's usefulness. It is best accompanied by readings or detailed explanations of Thai Buddhism.

Thai Images of the Buddha
  14 minutes, color, 16mm, 1962
  Sale $210.00, Rental $9.25
  Producer/Distributor: Indiana University
  Series: Arts of the Orient

Thai Images of the Buddha informatively traces the evolution of the Buddha image through various periods of Thai art history: Dvaravanti (sixth to eleventh), Lopburi (eleventh to fourteenth), Chieng Sen (twelfth to fourteenth), Sukhodaya (thirteenth to fifteenth), and Ayudhya (fifteenth to eighteenth). Based on the exhibition of Thai art which toured the United States from 1960 to 1962, this film is extensively supplemented by a catalogue, *The Arts of Thailand*, illustrating th : influence of Indian Gupta style on the images of the Dvaravati and of the Khmer (Cambodia) on Lopburi styles. Distinctive Thai contributions are highlighted by the famous Sukhodaya walking images of the Buddha.

Since it concentrates solely on Thai Buddhist sculptures without interspersing any other cultural material, the film will be of more value for courses in Southeast Asian art history than for the study of Theravada Buddhism as such. It is recommended for possible use together with the slide sets—*The Evolution of the Buddha Image, Story of the Buddha in Thai Murals*, and *Marks and Mudras of the Buddha*—as a means to discuss the relationship between the development of the Buddha image and the Buddha concept. For the early Buddhist aniconic tradition at Sanchi, see *The Glory That Remains*.

Thailand
  52 minutes, color, 16mm, 1979
  Sale $572.00, Rental $12.50
  Director: Arch Nicholson
  Series: Asian Insight (shown on Public Television as Views of Asia)
  Producer: John Temple
  Distributor: Australian Information Services

This surveys much of modern Thailand in its rural and urban settings, and attempts to explain the Thai people in terms of their concept of "Sanuk"—having a good time, taking it easy. Thai history is briefly surveyed with footage of the old capitals of Ayudha and Chiang Mai, with a discussion of the cultural mix of Thai, Chinese, and Malayan peoples.

The film begins with the statement, "Thailand has 200,000 Buddhist monks—they produce nothing". Buddhism and the monarchy are presented as the two major binding cultural factors uniting the Thai people. The narrative stresses the respect given to monks and the many layman who have entered the monastery for periods of three months or more. Besides expected scenes of the monk's begging rounds and public rituals, the film includes several minutes on the Buddhist response to modernization: a militant abbot exhorting his followers to work hard for modernization, and monks attending classes acquaint-ing them with government and private social welfare institutions.

The film has much to recommend it. The cinematography and range of scenery are both effective and the portrayal of Buddhism is generally sympathetic, albeit elementary. However, the film tends to highlight simplistic judgments ot he Thais as "a tolerant easy going people" and as "a nation of non-joiners." These characterizations are juxtaposed with questions about the extent to which the Thais will be able to learn from what are here referred to as the more vigorous cultures of the West.

Thailand: Land of Smiles
   27 minutes, color, 16mm, 1977
   Sale $425.00, Rental $42.50
   Producer: John Seabourne
   Series: World Cultural Geography Asian Notebook
   Distributor: Centron Educational Films
   Also available from: UIll

This film presents the traditional culture of Thailand: handicrafts, dance and festivals, rice production, silk weaving, and lumbering. The opening sequence treats Buddhism in Thailand by showing monks chanting and going on morning food rounds (pindapata) and temples in the Bangkok area. An elaborate guardian figure provides the transition to Thai classical dancing and painting based on the Ramayana at the Temple of the Emerald Buddha.

The second segment moves to northern Thailand and deals primarily with traditional methods of rice planting and harvesting, fishing, lumbering, silk production, pottery and silver handicrafts, as well as with the northern Thai fingernail dance. A third sequence

focuses on canal life within and around the Bangkok area, and the final
part of the film touches somewhat randomly on the historical ruins of
Ayudhya, dancing, boxing, cock fighting and bull fighting, and
concludes with Loi Krathong, the photogenic November festival of
lights.

The film provides a visually delightful look at selected aspects of
traditional Thai life and culture, but with limited attention to
Buddhism. Since it does not treat the effects of modernization, the film
is overly romanticized. Specifically, it refers to the Thai people as
peaceful and tranquil, and utilizes sequences (especially of the
dancing) which were obviously filmed at the Rose Garden, a tourist
center outside of Bangkok. Since it was made as a cultural geography
film, it is only marginally relevant to the study of Buddhism in
Southeast Asia. *Chiang Mai, Northern Capital* has more material on
Buddhist festivals and *Buddhism: Be Ye Lamps Unto Yourselves*
provides a better introduction to Thai Buddhism as such. Those
interested in dance might see *Hiraizumi: Capital of the North* (Noh
drama), *Buddhist Dances of Korea*.

Slides

L'Art Khmer
  2 volumes of 24 slides each
  Sale $36.00 per set
  **Producer: Jeannine Auboyer—Publications Filmée d'Art et
    d'Histoire**
  Distributor: Prothman Associates

These slides comprise a survey of Hindu and Buddhist temples and
statuary extant during the period of Indian colonization and influence
in Cambodia over the sixth to thirteenth centuries. The text (in French
with English summary) gives historical background and descriptions.
Volume One deals with the effloresence of the classical period and
includes views of Angkor Wat, Bantay Srei, and other monuments.
Volume Two includes Angkor Thom and other later monuments. The
booklet explains the importance of Hindu Kingship, the symbolism of
Hindu cosmology in the Mount Meru-style monuments, and examples of Hindu-Buddhist syncretism in the development of Cambodian
art and architecture. While the slide set is well conceived and the 150-
page French text provides a sound introduction to this period of
Cambodian art, the slides themselves are not of high quality. They are
generally brownish in color and all are not equally well photographed.

Buddhism in Southeast Asia and Ceylon
  220 slides, color
  Sale $80.00, Rental: $15.00
  Producer: Charles A. Kennedy
  Series: Asian Religions Media Resources
  Distributor: Visual Education Service, Yale Divinity School

This set of slides of the most wide-ranging collection available on Theravada Buddhism and Buddhism in Southeast Asia. The set is organized according to country: Burma (1-45), Ceylon (Sri Lanka - 46-95), Thailand (96-157), Laos (158-164), Cambodia (165-186), and Indonesia (180-220). A guide prepared by Charles A. Kennedy accompanies the collection with a brief opening statement about each country and its culture. The presentation focuses on both lay and monastic religious activities, although the slides for each country do not follow a logically developed outline. Included are festivals, temple and home rituals, meditation, famous Buddhist monuments, funeral ceremony, and contemporary developments within the Theravada sanghas.

The set as a whole, and the color quality in particular, is uneven. Nevertheless, this series represents a definite advance over the pioneering effort of Kenneth Morgan which focused largely on religious monuments. It is a useful tool for college-level classes in Buddhism and Asian religions.

The Story of the Buddha in Thai Murals
  20 slides, color, n.d.
  Sale $8.00
  Producer: Columbo Furio
  Distributor: New York University Asian Studies Curriculum Center

This set provides an overview of the life of the Buddha as depicted in Thai mural art from two sites (Wat Prathat in Chiang Mai and Buddhaisawan Temple in Bangkok) representing popular and classical styles. The Buddha's life is followed from the time of conception and Queen Maya's dream to the beginning of his ministry forty-nine days after his enlightenment. The set is useful for showing the supernatural and mythic qualities ascribed to the Buddha's life, and for comparing how greatly artistic representations may vary even within one Southeast Asian country. The slides are well chosen, the murals are attractive and visually interesting, and the photography is acceptable.

Recordings

The Music of Cambodia
UNESCO Collections—Musical Anthology of the Orient
Distributor: UNIPUB

Apparently, the only available selection of Buddhist Music from Cambodia is to be found on band 11 of this album. Band 11 lasts approximately five minutes, and is identified as "Prayer in Pali" sung by the ensemble of the monks of the Prayu Vongs Pagoda in Phnom Penh for the festival Meakka bochia. Psalmody on three notes derived from Indian Vedic Chant. The recording was made during a ceremony. Several hundred monks and laymen took part." The style is simple and archaic, with no similarity to the musical artistry of Southeast Asia.

The Music of Viet-Nam—I (The Tradition of Hue)
Recordings, Commentary, and Photographs by Tran Van Khe and Nguyen Huu Ba
UNESCO—A Musical Anthology of the Orient
Distributor: UNIPUB

This record has two bands of Vietnamese "folk" music that are Buddhist. The first is a recitation in Vietnamese Tung style (more like sing-song reading) from the *Suramgama Sutra*. The second, sung in more melodic Tan style, is on impermanence. No translations are given, and there is no discussion of the relationship between music and religion.

The notes are musicological, giving approximate transcriptions and discussions of musical styles and instruments.

The Music of Viet-Nam—II (South Viet-Nam)

This album refers in the notes repeatedly to record I, above. Band one, specifically on Buddhist music, contains more information than is available on record I. The Tan and Tung styles are compared within a brief selection from a funerary or memorial service. There is a call to bow three times and an invitation to prayer, followed by reading an unidentified text. Later bands include orchestral music which might accompany a ceremony as well as a theatrical production.

CHAPTER 4

Himalaya

Films

Bhutan—Land of the Peaceful Dragon
Himalayan Buddhism
A King Is Crowned
Ladakh
Lama Dances of Tibet
The Lama King
Meditation Crystallized
"Nepal: Land of the Gods" (see under Sherpa Legend, The Tantric Universe, and Tibetan Heritage)
Out of This World: Forbidden Tibet
A Prophecy (A Trilogy on Tibet)
The Religious Investiture of H.H. Dalai Lama
Requiem for a Faith
Sacred Art of Tibet
Sherpa High Country
Sherpa Legend
Tantra of Gyuto
The Tantric Universe
Tibetan Heritage
Tibetan Medicine: A Buddhist Approach to Healing
Tibetan Story

Slides

The Art of Tibet
Himalayan Art
Tibetan Art Set
Tibetan Buddhism

Recordings

The Music of Tibetan Buddhism
Tibetan Buddhism: The Ritual Orchestra and Chants
Tibetan Buddhist Rites from the Monasteries of Bhutan
Tibetan Mystic Song
Tibetan Songs of Gods and Demons—Ritual and Theatrical Music

Films

Bhutan—Land of the Peaceful Dragon
28 minutes, color, 16mm, n.d.
Sale none, Rental free
Commentary: Keith Shackleton
Producer: Franz Lazi Film (Stuttgart)
Distributor: Permanent Mission of Bhutan

This film surveys the Buddhist kingdom of Bhutan, its landscapes, architecture, arts and crafts, festivals, and elaborate Lamaistic rituals. Beginning with the road trip up the mountain gorges to Thimphu, the camera takes us through the streets, in and out of workshops and temples, and then moves out into the countryside to see how farming is carried on and to view a remarkable archery contest. The film shows the great monastic college of Bunaka Dzong and discusses the education of its monks. It then visits a beautiful mountain retreat, Tagtsang Gompa, and recounts its ancient history from the time of Padmasambhava. The film concludes with the great festival of Pharo, where the giant icon of Padmasambhava (claimed to be the world's largest thanka) is unfurled, and dances and processions are carried on for the entire day.

The film aims to encourage tourism to Bhutan and it succeeds admirably in showing the beauty and exotic nature of the previously inaccessible kingdom. It also chronicles much of Bhutanese life and religious activity that is relevant to the study of Buddhism, Asian religion, and culture.

Himalayan Buddhism
29 minutes, videocassette, color
Sale $45.00
Director: and Host: David M. Knipe
Lecturer: Stephan Beyer
Series: Exploring the Religions of South Asia
Distributor: University of Wisconsin South Asia Center

This videocassette provides an illustrated lecture on Tibetan Buddhism conveying considerable information on the history and culture of Tibet. The Indian Buddhist background is sketched, illustrated with color stills of the ruins of Nalanda and other Buddhist sites. The lecturer next considers the dissemination of Buddhism into Tibet, its interaction with the native shamanistic religion, the stories of the great missionaries Padmasambhava and Atisha, and lastly, the appearance of four Sects: Nyingma, Kagyu, Sakya, and Gelug. It concludes with a discussion of Tibetan rituals, showing Tibetan artifacts and slides of ritual objects such as thread-crosses, torma offerings, and so forth.

There are serious flaws in this lecture, the most unfortunate being Beyer's failure to distinguish between high and popular levels of Tibetan religion. Thus, the fact that Tibetan Buddhism preserves the whole range of literary, philosophical, and artistic traditions of Indian Buddhism is overlooked, and semi-shamanistic rituals are said to be the "end to which all other functions are subsumed." The impression conveyed is that Tibetans are "primitive," steeped in magic, and filled with aggression—e.g., engage in beating the young monks or debating ferociously.

Due to its bias toward the "demon-worshipping" stereotype of Tibetan Buddhism, the videocassette cannot be recommended as an introduction to this religious tradition.

A King is Crowned
33 minutes, color, 16mm, 1974
Sale India only, Rental free
Producer: Shanti Varma, Films Division, Government of India
Distributor: Permanent Mission of Bhutan

This officially commissioned film depicts the coronation of the present king of Bhutan, Jigme Singye Wangchuk, at Thimphu on June 2, 1974. It opens with scenic shots of the Bhutanese countryside, and then shows the capital city of Thimphu, and the monumental stupa to world peace constructed by the present king's father. The scene shows preparation for the coronation, with the decoration of the city and the main monastery temple, the arrival of Asian and Western dignitaries. The ceremony itself is then portrayed with good detail, showing the elements of the Bhutanese version of Buddhist kingship in a fascinating way, and emphasizing the relations between the secular and religious orders in the country. The film concludes with the coronation parade and royal speech, with the various national dances of Bhutan and their reflection of Indo-Tibetan-Nepalese syncretism shown at length.

The print seen for this review was of poor quality, although the basic cinematography was good. The commentary is clear and informative, although it emphasizes a somewhat modernistic bias, and systematically underplays the Tibetan mainstream of the Bhutanese heritage.

Ladakh
15 minutes, color, 16mm, 1963
Sale India only (To purchase, contact Government of India Films Division listed in appendix of distributors), Rental free
Director: Shanti Varma
Producer: K. L. Khandpur
Distributor: Information Services of India

This film presents an Indian Government view of Ladakh. Most of the film portrays geography and agriculture and focuses on a young couple who evidently symbolize "young Ladakh." Portions of the film do show a number of the impressive monasteries, a puja performed by the high Lama of Ladakh, Kushok Bakula, (who is not introduced by name), and a set of festival dances at Hemis monastery performed in celebration of Padmasambhava's conquest of the local deities of Tibet to make the land a haven for Mahayana Buddhism.

The film provides decent color footage of this recently accessible region. Unfortunately, the quality of the print viewed was quite poor. Due to its modernistic bias, the film makes no effort to present Himalayan culture on its own terms. There is little exploration of Buddhism, or real appreciation of the treasures contained in the extensive monasteries.

Lama Dances of Tibet
   42 minutes, color, 16mm
   Sale inquire from distributor
   Producer: Virendra Kumar Jain
   Distributor: Navin Kuman, Inc.

This film shows Tibetan *"Gar 'Chams"* ritual dances, filmed at the Tashi Jong Monastic Community at Palapur in Himachal Pradesh, North India, where the Khamtrul Rinpoche has preserved authentically the tradition of these dances. Studied in particular were the dances of the Gesar epic drama, including dance portrayals of tiger, snow lion, garuda, and dragon, showing the two-man animal dance technique. The black hat dances are also depicted in slow detail, as are solemn dances of dakinis and dakas. Very colorful, the film gives the viewer the opportunity to study the costumes and movements of the dancers in detail.

There is no narration, and the only explanation given is in titles flashed occasionally on the screen. Despite the technical excellence of this film, the pace is slow and might be boring for the general audience. It is useful for a class in which ritual dances of Asia in general, or of the Buddhist communities in particular, are under consideration, although a knowledgeable commentary would have to be supplied by the instructor. Used in connection with *Sherpa High Country,* the Bhutanese *A King Is Crowned,* or *The Lama King,* it would give viewers a long look at the festival dancing of the Tibetans.

The Lama King
   52 minutes, color, 16mm, 1976 (Footage from 1950s)
   Sale inquire, BBC London, Rental $75.00

Producer: Vanya Kewley for BBC
Distributor: Office of Tibet

This film is a study of His Holiness, the Fourteenth Dalai Lama, at his headquarters in the Himalayan foothills in Dharmsala, India. It emphasizes his human qualities but explores in depth the complex religious and political dimensions of his office. Beginning with a ceremony in the newly built Thekchen Choling temple, the film returns to Tibet for a survey of recent events showing the Dalai Lama in Tibet, the Chinese invasion, and events leading to his escape to India in 1959. Chinese atrocities and genocidal policies are more honestly chronicled than in any other film on this subject.

Returning to Dharmsala, we follow His Holiness in his daily routine, beginning at 4 A.M. with a light breakfast, followed by morning prayer and meditation, including repeated offering of the universe as mandala. This is followed by an interview in English. The next sequence moves to the Nursery and the role of the Tibetan children in preserving Tibetan culture. Tibetan arts and crafts are shown by the refugee community. A second interview with His Holiness then touches on the issue of his attitude toward the Chinese occupants of Tibet, wherein he gives a moving address on the Buddhist teaching of love and respect for one's enemy.

The long final sequence depicting the events of a New Year's celebration is unique in that each ritual is clearly labelled and briefly but accurately explained. The deities visualized and invoked are shown in well-chosen artworks. There is an intermission in this sequence for a third interview in which His Holiness makes some interesting observations on religion in general and about the future of the Dalai Lama institution.

This is the best available film on the Dalai Lama and on the Tibetan refugee community in India, as well as one of the best so far on Tibetan Buddhism in general, and is recommended for classroom use and general audiences.

Meditation Crystallized
   13 minutes, color, 16mm, 1973
   Sale $200.00, Rental $25.00
   Producer: Irving and Elda Hartley
   Distributor: Hartley Films Foundation
   Also available from: UIowa

This film is a combination of Lama Anagarika Govinda's authoritative and lucid explanation of the nature and function of some fine examples of Tibetan Buddhist sacred art, and a contrived cinematography that is sometimes annoying. Lama Govinda, in his gentle and compelling way, clearly explains the function of art in Tibetan

Buddhism in connection with the meditative training, showing how the vivid deities represent not "demons" or "angels" but the crystallizations of states of awareness attained by the spiritual practitioner. He discusses the function of a mandala and comments upon the potential usefulness of these techniques in Western psychology and religion. M~st memorable is his interpretation of the awesome dieties such as Shri Devi as representations of the "death of ego prior to illumination."

This film is recommended for its record of Lama Govinda's discussion and the accompanying works of art. It could be used with *Tibetan Heritage, Sacred Art of Tibet,* and films on Zen aesthetics in a section of a course on meditational aesthetics.

Out of This World: Forbidden Tibet
82 minutes, color, 16mm, 1951(?)
Sale none, Rental $35.00
Narrator: Lowell Thomas, Sr. and Jr.
Distributor: Audio Brandon Films

This film contains some of the best footage available of the old Tibet. Told in a personal, entertaining, although dated manner, the film recounts the trip to Tibet of the two famous newscasters, Lowell Thomas and his son, at the invitation of His Holiness the Dalai Lama in 1950 when the Tibetans first began to take the Chinese invasion seriously and appealed to the outside world for help. Footage of the Gangtok-Lhasa mule and yak caravan shows the beauty and ruggedness of the Himalayan foothills and passes, and the stark quality of the Tibetan plateau. Scenes filmed in Gyangtse at the great stupa, as well as street scenes of the people in their colorful attire going on their daily business, are fascinating. The footage of Lhasa shows the bustle of the bazaar and the interaction of the lay people with the monks. The Potala towers are shown in the distance, although unfortunately there is no footage from within it. ∴so documented are the great cathedral of Lhasa, Drepung, Sera, and Nechung monasteries. The film climaxes with a visit to a summer festival at the Norbu Lingka summer palace of the Dalai Lama. There is an audience with the fifteen-year-old ruler, his first public film appearance of that sort.

The rather homespun Tibetan army is filmed on parade, and some rather touching appeals from the diplomatic officer Liushar are made for world protection against the Chinese incursions extremely poignant when viewed now after thirty years of suffering by the Tibetan people under occupation and in exile.

The cinematic quality of this film is good. The commentary is on a popular level so that very little reliable information about Tibetan culture or religion is conveyed. In fact, the old misleading stereotypes ("Tibetan religion is a mixture of Buddhism and devil-worship") are confidently perpetuated. Contradictory facts abound about population, censuses, the role of monasticism, the poor distribution of wealth, and the class system. The usual modernistic contempt for the "backward" country is clearly manifest in much of the commentary, some occasional perceptive remarks notwithstanding. In sum, this is a worthwhile film to bring Tibet to life, but it should be accompanied by corrective commentary.

A Prophecy
   64 minutes, color, 16mm, 1978
   Sale inquire from distributor
   Director: Graham Coleman
   Series: A Trilogy on Tibet: Time Before, Time Being, Time After (Part I)
   Producer: David Lascelles
   Distributor: Thread Cross Films and University of California— Berkeley, Extension Media Center

The first of a series of three films on the Tibetan community in exile in India, this film is a montage of scenes from life in the refugee community around the Sera Monastery in Karnataka state, South India, as well as the Tibetan government in exile headquarters in Dharmsala in the Himalayas, home of His Holiness the Dalai Lama. A Tibetan lay family is studied in its daily religious and ordinary activity, and the Sera monks are shown in their studies, practicing traditional debates on religious matters, and painting and building their new temple and monastic hall. In Dharmsala, His Holiness is shown giving a public audience to a number of lay persons and children. Then a carpet-weaving collective is shown with people at work together in this ancient craft. In the next segment, the Dalai Lama gives teachings on the *Guhyasamaja Tantra* to a group of monks. Returning to Sera, we witness preparations and execution of a Hayagriva consecration by the Abbot for the community at large, as well as lay religious observances of circumambulation and praying around the village stupa. The film concludes with the Dalai Lama's March 10th speech in Dharmsala on the anniversary of the tragic attempt at revolution against the Chinese invasion in 1959.

This film is excellent cinematically, and includes some of the best available footage on the life of the Tibetan lay community in exile. Its portrayal of the debating is also vivid and well narrated, as is its coverage of some of the prayers and rituals and its study of the economic realities of refugee life. By accurate and correct translation, it manages to give a proper idea of what is taking place in the activities of the monks and lay people, and does not seek to exploit the subject for commercial titillation of the Western audience. Its one drawback is a somewhat loose overall structure, leaving a final impression of a collage of interesting scenes, and no overall message. The title is never therefore clearly explained, and one is left wondering who prophesied what. However, this is still one of the most useful films yet produced on Tibetans and Tibetan Buddhism. Used together with *The Lama King, Tantra of Gyuto, Tibetan Heritage*, and perhaps *Out of This World: Forbidden Tibet*, with its footage of Tibet proper, it would contribute to a good cinematic documentation of Tibetan Buddhism.

The Religious Investiture of H.H. The Dalai Lama
   14 minutes, color, 16mm, 1959
   Sale $220.00, Rental $30.00
   Director: Jigme Taring
   Distributor: Office of Tibet

This film contains unique footage filmed in 1959 by Jigme Taring of the doctoral examinations of His Holiness the Fourteenth Dalai Lama conducted at Ganden monastery and the Jokhang cathedral in Lhasa. It begins with a colorful procession of His Holiness and entourage from Lhasa to the Ganden monastery. After the philosophical debates are concluded, the party goes out into the nearby hills where audiences are granted to the masses in an ornate tent set up for the occasion. There follows a sequence of footage in the Jokhang (with further debates), followed by a festival of celebratory dances given in the courtyard by Lama dancers.

This film shows the nature of the Dalai Lama institution in Tibet, and details the Tibetan hierarchy and its mores. Due to its brevity, it should be used in conjunction with *The Lama King, Out of This World: Forbidden Tibet*, or *Tantra of Gyuto* for a more complete picture of the Dalai Lama and recent Tibetan Buddhism.

Requiem For A Faith
   27 minutes, color, 16mm, 1968
   Sale $300.00, Rental $35.00
   Producer: Irving and Elda Hartley
   Writer/Narrator: Huston Smith
   Distributor: Hartley Film Foundation
   Also available from: UCB, FlaSt, UIowa, UIll, UMich, UMinn, UNoCar, SyrU PennSt, BYU, UWash, UWisc

This film depicts the life of the Tibetan refugees in North India, focusing on their festivals, arts, religious beliefs, and rituals. The film refers to the uniqueness of Tibetan culture as a last vestige of an archaic, medieval civilization, and thus presents the scenes from Northern India as remnants of this civilization, for which the film purports to be a "requiem." There are excellent sequences of Tibetan dancing, both folk and religious, good scenes of carpet weaving, woodblock carving and printing, thanka painting, spring incense rituals, and recurrent sequences of an elderly yogi meditating. Buddhist doctrine is rendered by Prof. Smith in an impressionistic but vivid way, presenting the Tibetan concern with escape from the painful cycles of samsara as the reason for their lack of concern with technology and material culture of modernity. There is a concluding sequence of a Tantric ritual performed by the Gyume Tantric College, with chanting performed in multi-toned voice by the monks. The film concludes with a lament for the loss of the "living faith" of Tibet proper, and an affirmation of "perennial philosophy" as being present at the core of all surviving faiths.

On balance, however, the film is worthwhile as a cinematic catalogue of Tibetan ways as preserved in exile.

Regrettably, this film uses gimicky special effects: mantras and mandalas whirling around to symbolize samsara, with the Tibetan letters unfortunately turned on their sides.

Sacred Art of Tibet
   31 minutes, color, 16 mm, 1972
   Sale $300.00, Rental $35.00
   Producer: Larry Jordan
   Distributor: Hartley Film Foundation
   Also available from: Purdue

This film is a "psychedelic" treatment of Tibetan iconic art (thanka), complete with variegated special effects, electronic music, and poor narrative. It provides a rich panoply of iconic forms, using images and paintings, of Shakyamuni, Amitabha, Avalokiteshvara, Tara, Vajrapani, Padmasambhava, Manjushri Yamantaka, Vajrasattva Mahakala, Rahu, Gesar, and the Wheel of Life (bhavacakra) diagram so common in Tibet.

It is deliberately exciting and visually provocative, but may be offensive or overwhelming to some. Its commentary is not well informed, and it does not really explain to the viewer what is being seen. The special effects frequently seem gimmicky and contrived. Recommended for general audiences in search of something unusual, but not useful for students who have more solid access to this art. The sacred art of Tibet is more accurately described in *Meditation Crystallized, Tibetan Heritage,* or some of the slide sets on Tibetan art.

Sherpa High Country
   20 minutes, color, 16mm, 1976
   Sale $285.00, Rental $29.00
   Producer: Xenia Lisanevich
   Distributor: University of California—Berkeley

This film portrays scenes from the spectacular Himalayan country-side around Solo Kumbu region below Mt. Everest, showing the Sherpas in their daily round, working as porters for mountain expeditions, herding yaks, farming, and trading in impromptu bazaars. The central sequence is filmed at Thyangboche Monastery, the highest in the world at 15,000 feet, in which a New Year's festival is pictured in some detail. Dances of humorous, legendary, and exorcistic types are shown in a leisurely and comprehensible way.

This film has excellent cinematography and authentic coverage of an authentic folk festival coupled with a clear, sympathetic, and well-informed commentary. Lack of a live soundtrack mars some of the rituals for the expert, although the dubbed-in soundtrack made from archival recordings is adequate as a substitute device.

Sherpa Legend
  21 minutes, color, 16mm, 1976
  Sale $290.00, Rental $50.00
  Producer: Sheldon Rochlin
  Series: Nepal Land of the Gods
  Distributor: Focus International, Inc.

This film is the third of a three-part series, "Nepal: Land of the Gods." It attempts to convey the feeling of the high Himalayas, along with the religious and cultural atmosphere of the Sherpa people. It opens with aerial footage of snow peaks and the remote monastic town of Namche Bazaar. A sequence of town and fireplace scenes with the Sherpas and their visitors are strung on the thread of stories about the famous yeti, "abominable snowman." Some temple scenes are shown with a Sherpa Lama performing some ritual chants in the exorcistic mode, with a discussion of Padmasambhava, demons, and "dakini"— angels. The film concludes with a rather eerie, if somewhat theatrical sequence of a Lama waving his ritual staff at spirits he appears to sense above an exquisite turquoise glacial lake.

This film would be better with more attention to authentic ritual and folk scenes, and less magic and mystery. The interesting subject of Himalayan shamanism and its relationship to Tibetan Buddhism is implied, but its sensationalism and lack of information and insight unfortunately leave the issue more clouded than ever. It is recommended for the Himalayan scenery and as an ethnographic record, but only of limited usefulness in courses on Buddhism (the least useful in the trilogy).

Tantra of Gyuto
  52 minutes (2 reels), color, 16mm, 1975
  Sale $690.00, Rental $80.00

Director: Sheldon Rochlin (New Line Cinema)
Producer: Allied Artists London & Snowlion Communications
Distributor: Focus International, Inc.

Celebrating the five hundredth anniversary of the founding of Gyuto Tantric College in Lhasa, Tibet, in 1474, a group of monks led by the Abbot Tara Tulku came from Dalhousie, India, their residence at that time, to perform some of their major ceremonies in London. This film gives the fullest coverage available of an Unexcelled (Anuttara) Yoga Tantra mandala ceremony, beginning with the monks' circumambulating the powder-mandala of the Sri Guhya Samaja Tantra, chanting in their unique multi-tonal style, accompanied by bells, cymbals, and horns. The scene then shifts back to Dalhousie, showing a painter, weavers, mandala-makers, and monks in morning prayers and debates. The former abbot presents good-luck scarves to Tara Tulku and the departing monks, and they all set out for London, first by jeep and then by plane, symbolizing their entrance into the "modern world." The scene then fades back again in time to the history of Tibet, using some remarkable old footage of the rugged countryside, Tibetans in medieval warrior costume, some paintings of historical figures such as the early Kings and Padmasambhava, an Indian missionary. The Dalai Lama is shown taking his examinations at Ganden and the Jo Khang in Lhasa, the Potala, his remarkable palace, is also portrayed. Finally, there is a sequence showing the Chinese occupation and the flight of the Dalai Lama to India in 1959. This sequence concludes with the Gyuto monks arriving and being greeted in London. There is a sequence of the Dalai Lama discussing the ceremony, which, mysteriously, is not translated or even summarized in the English narrative. In the second reel, the film dwells at length on the Yamantaka consecration, filled with stirring chanting and colorful costumes, with the Tibetan long-horns, bells, and cymbals being used to good effect. There is a concluding section of awesome rites performed to propitiate the terrifying protector, Mahakala.

Overall the film is an effective immersion in the world of Tibetan religion. The commentary is sometimes quite good, with a minimum of misinformed or confusing information. The content ranges quite widely, yet it is imaginatively structured and the viewer can keep his bearings easily. At times, the ceremonies become somewhat monotonous, but often authentic art is interspersed to give an idea of what the celebrants are visualizing during the phases of the rites. The film is recommended for general audiences as well as for students of Tibetan Buddhism. Buddhism in general, Tantra, religious ritual, or comparative religion. It can be used effectively with the trilogy, Nepal: Land of the Gods; or it can be used with *Torches of Todaiji* for cross-cultural comparative ritual study. Further, this film provides an excellent introduction to Tibetan music.

The Tantric Universe
   22 minutes, color, 16mm, 1976
   Sale $290.00, Rental $50.00
   Producer: Sheldon Rochlin
   Series: Nepal: Land of the Gods
   Distributor: Focus International, Inc.

This film is the second of a three-part series, "Nepal: Land of the Gods." It provides a cinematically vivid treatment of the physical, human, and religious landscape of the Kathmandu valley. It opens with unique footage of a ritual conducted by Nepali Vajracaryas (Buddhist practitioners) at a forest stupa, accompanied by a brief account of the cosmogonic myths of the region. The film then jumps to the present King of Nepal, and the bustle of downtown Kathmandu, with its ancient architecture and street shrines.

An extensive portrayal of the Matsyendranath temple shows the Hindu-Buddhist syncretism that marks religion in Nepal, although the narrative is hard-pressed to keep pace with the succession of images. Subsequently the film deals with the Pashupatinath temple sacred to Shiva, artistic depictions of the mother goddess, Shakti, in her terrifying representation as Kali, and graphic treatment of a blood sacrifice.

The final section switches back to Buddhism, discussing the Buddhist view of the feminine principle in the cosmos, the role of sexual imagery in Tantric practice, and the mythology of Padmasambhava, with some attempt at philosophical explanation. At the conclusion there is a return to the original scene of the Tantric ritual conducted by the Vajracaryas.

The film succeeds in communicating the exotic atmosphere of Kathmandu and the religions of Nepal. Its narrative is somewhat marred by a tendency to grand generalizations regarding the "illusory nature of the world," "alternative realities," and so on. The cinematography tends toward sensationalism at times, but is effective nonetheless. While it is to be recommended for classroom or independent viewing, it would be most effective if accompanied by careful commentary. This film may be profitably used in conjunction with its companion films in the series— *Tibetan Heritage* and *Sherpa Legend*, or with other films listed in the index under "Himalaya," "Tantra," and "Syncretism."

Tibetan Heritage
   19 minutes, color, 16 mm, 1976
   Sale $290.00, Rental $50.00
   Producer: Sheldon Rochlin
   Series: Nepal: Land of the Gods
   Distributor: Focus International, Inc.

This film is one of a three-part series, "Nepal: Land of the Gods," and documents life in a Tibetan monastery in Nepal, the newly built Kagyu Shedrub Ling of the Karma Kagyu sect at Bodnath in the Kathmandu valley. The cinematography is excellent, and the narration well informed and interesting. A number of monastic assemblies are shown with colorful scenes of liturgy and prayer. Young novice Lamas are depicted in their studies and play, and some of the basic ethical and philosophical teachings are accurately recounted. The religious history and cosmology of the sect is explained and illustrated from Tibetan paintings, with depictions of scenes from the Buddha's life, portraits of Maitreya, Manjushri, Avalokiteshvara, the Wheel of Life and the six realms of being, and Padmasambhava. Shots of the giant stupa of Bodhnath show the surrounding community with some attention given to the relations between lay and monastic communities.

The film shows the distinctive character of Tibetan Buddhism, and is particularly effective in showing the upbringing and education of a young Tibetan monks, not only through mood and setting, but also in explaining the basic doctrines that they study. This film is recommended for classroom use or general viewing. For other films on monastic training, see *Zen in Life, Buddhism: Be Ye Lamps Unto Yourselves*. For other films on Buddhist art, see *Buddhist Art, Sacred Art of Tibet, Meditation Crystallized*.

Tibetan Medicine: A Buddhist Approach to Healing
35 minutes, color, 16mm, 1976
Sale $25.00, Rental $35.00
Director: Sheldon Rochlin and Mikki Maher
Producer: Hartley Productions
Distributor: Hartley Film Foundation

This film is a cinematic documentation of a day in the busy life and practice of the Tibetan woman doctor, Losang Dolma, formerly one of the physicians at His Holiness the Dalai Lama's medical center in Dharmsala, India. Dr. Dolma is seen diagnosing patients, prescribing Tibetan remedies for them, and reading the deep pulses in the wrist from which the Tibetan physician "senses" the condition of the inner organs. Then follows a sequence about medical education, with an overvoice description of the "Four Tantras" which form the basic texts for Tibetan medicine. Next comes a beautiful sequence of an herb-gathering expedition up into the Himalayas, showing the herbs, flowers, minerals, and animal products from which the medicines are compounded. Finally, the traditional Tibetan surgical tools are displayed and a moxibustion treatment is shown, as well as a heated golden needle treatment given to the filmmaker.

The film is useful for its depiction of the medical center and the

Tibetan refugee community, as a portrait of the remarkable Dr. Dolma and as a record of the relation between Buddhism and medicine. However, it conveys a confusing picture of Tibetan medicine itself, being impressionistic and sensationalistic rather than scholarly and informative. There is a confused overlay of spiritualism and shamanistic healing practices which obscures the basically empirical and scientific bent of the Tibetan medical tradition.

Tibetan Story
  32 minutes, color, 16mm, 1965
  Sale none, Rental $30.00
  Director: P. Garland
  Producer: M. K. Johns for Libertas Films
  Distributor: Office of Tibet

This film emphasizes the Chinese invasion of Tibet and the wholesale oppression of the Tibetan people; including systematic suppression of Tibetan Buddhism which followed the Chinese take-over of Tibet in 1959. Somewhat emotionally intense in its treatment of these issues, the tone of moral outrage nevertheless stays well grounded in documentary footage. It shows highly emotional scenes such as Chinese soldiers burning sacred scriptures, and women and elderly persons dead in the snows of the passes along the escape route to India. The Tibetan communities in India—in Mussoorie, Dharmsala, Darjeeling, and Mysore—are also shown in their struggle to preserve Tibetan culture.

There is an interesting scene of a conversation between the Dalai Lama and an eminent Christian spokesman concerning the meeting and mutual respect of the major world religions in the secular climate of the present age. Parallels are drawn between the Buddhist idea of compassion and Christian love.

This set was based on a 1970 art exhibition which drew on a number agony of exile, and depicting the way in which Buddhists of Tibet endured such difficulties.

Slides

The Art of Tibet
  39 slides, 1970
  Sale $30.00
  Producer: Pratapaditya Pal
  Exhibited at: Asia House Gallery
  Distributor: Interook

This set was based on a 1970 art exhibition which drew on a number of Western collections. The slides include twenty thankas, seventeen metallic images and two manuscript pages from a *Prajna Paramita* manuscript. The art objects have been chosen for their beauty and art-historical significance, and the slides effectively capture their attractiveness. The one- or two-paragraph descriptions of each slide contain some basic information about the deities, saints, etc., portrayed in the art. However, the text concentrates on the aesthetic appeal rather than the religious significance of the art. For example: "Especially intriguing are the deeply expressive eyes with their darting yet penetrating gaze."

Himalayan Art
100 slides (1801–1900) color with separate list of identifications
Distributor: American Committee on South Asian Art

Only half of this set is pertinent to the study of Buddhism, but this half (slides 1851-1900) represents an unusual selection of slides taken in Buddhist monasteries in Ladakh, North India. The principal sites shown include Alchi Monastery (slides 1862-1888), Phyang Monastery (slides 1855-56, 1896-1900), and Bazgo Monastery (slides 1889-1895). Each site has its own distinct style of paintings, and the photography captures some of the beautiful paintings on the monastery interiors. Unfortunately, these slides have even less than the usual minimal identification supplied in the ACSAA series. Paintings are simply identified according to what building they were found in, with no mention of what is depicted.

Tibetan Art Set
100 slides, n.d., color
Sale $100.00
Compiler: John C. Huntington
Photographers: John C. and Susan Huntington
Distributor: American Committee on South Asian Art

This important visual resource shows a good selection of well photographed Tibetan religious art. Sculpture (slides 1-29) and paintings (slides 59-100) make up the bulk of the set. These are mainly arranged according to the styles of different geographic regions, except for slides 88-100 which have been added to show some essential iconographic features. The sculpture and paintings do show a variety of Buddhas, Arhats, monks, Mahasiddhas, and other beings in benign and awesome aspects in a well-balanced display, and all are clearly identified as to what they represent, and where and when they originated. Slides 30-57 show ritual objects and the offering of materials such as vajras, phur-pas (ritual daggers), a mandala, an amulet box (three-dimensional, open and closed), a chaitya, and a skull bowl. Of special interest are nine unusual slides (46-54) showing details of ornate and colorful butter-sculpture offerings on which is displayed a veritable cosmos of divine and mortal beings.

Tibetan Buddhism
  100 slides, n.d., mostly color
  Sale $40.00, Rental $10.00
  Text: Nathan Katz
  Editor/Collector: Charles A. Kennedy
  Series: Asian Religions Media Resources
  Distributor: Visual Education Service, Yale Divinity School

This is the fifth set in the Asian Religion and Media Resources Series. It is based primarily on the archives and art collection of the Newark Museum and draws on the expertise of Curator Valrae Reynolds and Curator Emeritus Eleanor Olson. The text and slides provide a good overview of Tibetan cultural history and geography, and uses rare photos from early expeditions to Tibet sponsored by the Newark Museum. The art and ritual objects are appropriately chosen and described. Of special interest are a painting of the Wheel of Life (slides 21-25), a section on altars and ritual instruments, and a brief discussion of the Tibetan Pantheon (slides 84-91). The slides are well chosen and the text is generally clear and reliable. However, only a few sects of Tibetan Buddhism are discussed in depth. Ritual objects are shown, but their use is not indicated, and the discussion of the pantheon with slides of yab-yum figures and terrifying aspects is not clearly developed.

Recordings

The Music of Tibetan Buddhism
  3 records (1965)
  Records, Notes, Photographs by Peter Crosely Hollard
  UNESCO Collection—Musical Anthology of the Orient #9, 10, 11.
  Distributor: UNIPUB

These records, based on taping sessions in May and June of 1961, attempt to give a comprehensive overview of Tibetan Buddhist music. Each album comes with several pages of notes in English, French, and German giving brief musicological descriptions of the excerpts with minimum historical or religious background. The recordings include performances by monks from four different major sects: Nyinmapa, Kagyudpa, Sakyapa and Gelugpa.

Record one is especially noteworthy for its inclusion of music of the Nyinmapa monasteries in Sikkim, including praises of Guru Padmasambhava (comparable to recordings on *Tibetan Buddhist Rites from the Monasteries of Bhutan*). Record one includes an introduction to the orchestra with eight bands devoted to examples of solo playing by different instruments. Side two is recordings by the Kagyudpa sect, including morning and evening music for shyams and trumpets and two vocal sections, one sung by monks and laity.

Record two has recordings of the Sakyapa sect and the Gelugpa sect. Side one includes recitations from the "History of the Sakya Religion" and a musical offering of thanks. Side two records passages from the Gelugpa sect which is headed by the Dalai Lama. Of special interest are a prayer for the Dalai Lama sung by a single monk, melodic recitation from the Lamrim and a choral and orchestral offering asking for purification from sin.

The record *Tibet III* contains more recordings from the Kagyudpa and Gelugpa sects. Side one includes "Praises of the Goddess Tara" (lektima) in a different rendition from that on the recording *Tibetan Songs of Gods and Demons . . . .* Side two is devoted entirely to a recording of an important prayer ascribed to Tsongkapa, the founder of the sect.

Tibetan Buddhism: The Ritual Orchestra and Chants
  Recorded by David Lewiston (1976)
  Notes by David Lewiston and Lobrang Lhalongpa
  Distributor: Nonesuch Records (#H72071)

This recording was made at the Tashi Jong refugee center in northern India, where monks of the Drukpa Teagyu sect have established a new monastery. The record involves three sectons, a beautifully sung choral invocation of Padmasambhava with rhythmic bell and drum accompaniment (15 minutes) and two Porteors of an invocation of Mahakala. The notes give a clear, simple explanation of the function of music in Tibetan Tantric Buddhism, and background information on the liturgies. For other performances of Mahakala invocations by a different sect, compare this album with *Tantra of Gyuto-Mahakala* and *The Music of Tibet* (not reviewed in this volume).

Tibetan Buddhist Rites from the Monasteries of Bhutan
  4 volumes, n.d.
  Recorded by John Levy with extensive notes
  Distributor: Lyrichord Records (LLST 7255-56-57-58)

These four records provide a valuable survey of the styles of Tibetan Buddhist music preserved in the monasteries of the Buddhist kingdom of Bhutan. Each album comes with six pages of well-written, descriptive notes, translations, and photographs, including two-and-a-half pages of background information on Bhutan and Tibetan music.

Vol. 1: Rituals of the Drukpa Order from Thimphu and Runakha.
The recordings on this album are all performed by lay monks of the Drukpa Kagyupa Order. Portions of the daily morning services are on side one, band one (Propitiation of the Dharma Pala or Guardian of the Dharma Genyen); band three (Exhortation of the Dharma Pala, Goddess of Long Life); and side two, band two, (Aspiration To Be Reborn in Amitabha's Western Paradise). Other passages in this recording include invocations of Mahakala, Mahamudra, Amitayus, and prayers to the three Buddha bodies of the Lamas and for the long life of the Lama prior to receiving spiritual instructions. Side two, bands five to eight are melodic tunes chanted by nuns. The notes include translations of most of the chants and description of the instrumental accompaniment.

Vol. 2: Sacred Dances and Rituals of the Nyingmapa and Drukpa Orders, Recorded at Nyimalung and Tangsa.
Side one records ritual dances with good descriptive notes and photographs. Bands three, four, and five are of special interest, describing part of the performances of the four-day dance worship of Guru Padmasambhava. The five bands on side two include three further invocations of Padmasambhava and two pieces for shawms (double-reed trumpets), one calling down the deities, the other a folk melody.

Vol. 3: Temple Rituals and Public Ceremonies
Side one has three selections from a Nyingmapa rite of Great Perfection (Tibetan Drubchen, Sanskrit Mahasiddhi) and two semi-secular dance songs. Side two has music from a popular temple dance festival and three interesting chants performed by manips (wandering ministrel, religious ascetics).

Vol. 4: Tibetan Bhutanese Instrumental and Folk Music
This album contains a pilgrim song and a folk dance/song in praise of the dharma, but is primarily useful for ethnographic background.

Tibetan Mystic Song
  Sung by Abbots of the Brug Pa Bkabrayed sect
  No notes or recording credits
  Distributor: Lyrichord Records (LLST 7290)

This recording inexplicably includes no printed information what-soever! The photos on the front and back of the album have virtually no relationship to the recording. The label on the record identifies the bands including sixteen songs by Milarepa and other poet saints of Tibet.

The singing itself is expert. Leaders of Milarepas lineage perform solos and duets without accompaniment. The recording gives a good sense of the range of rhythms and melodic and vocal styles in Tibetan religious song.

Tibetan Songs of Gods and Demons—Ritual and Theatrical Music Recording, notes and photographs by Stephan Beyer Distributor: Lyrichord Records (LLST 7291)

Side two of this recording is especially useful for the study of Tibetan Buddhist music. Band one gives the Praises of the Goddess Tara in twenty-one stanzas, which is known by virtually all Tibetan monks and laity. Here a single monk chants. Band two gives a selection from the beginning of a chod (life-cutting) ritual in which the practioner symbolically offers up his own body. A full translation is available in *Tibetan Strange and Secret Doctrines*. Band three is a dialogue poem from the life of Milarepa. The recording includes three pages of closely written notes. The three bands are given with complete translations and clear and useful notes on their religious importance. A trans-literated Tibetan text may be ordered from Lyrichord.

The final band is of orchestral accompaniment to rituals com-memorating the gurus. Side one provides a theatrical performance of a piece called "Lotus Blazing Light" and a passage from the Epic of Gesar.

CHAPTER 5

China

Films

The Ancient Chinese
Buddhism in China*
China: The Golden Age
China: The Great Cultural Mix
China: The Heavenly Khan
Chinese Legends, Gods and Prophets
Chinese Sculpture through the Ages
Journey into the Night: Chinese Funeral Rites

Slides

Chinese Religions

Recordings

Chinese Buddhist Music

*Reviewed under Section I: General and Historical Introductions

Films

The Ancient Chinese
24 minutes, color, 16mm, 1974
Sale $380.00, Rental $38.00
Director/Writer: Philip Strapp
Producer: Julien Bryan
Distributor: International Film Foundation, Inc.
Also available from: UCol, UIll, UIowa, UNeb, KentSt, UWisc, UWY

This film presents a sweeping survey of the Chinese people, their land, and history. It includes a brief account of the Buddhist penetration into China, its background in Indian Buddhism, and its flowering in China up to the persecutions in the ninth century A.D.

The pace is quite fast throughout this film, and there is an unfortunate lack of maps and diagrams to orient the viewer in the bewildering array of art, historical eras, landscapes, and monuments. While generally Sino-centric, it does make several helpful comparisons to Western civilization. In general, this film is better than most in the field and therefore is recommended as an introduction to Chinese civilization either for independent learning or classroom use.

China: The Golden Age
23 minutes, color, 16mm, 1977
Sale $280.00, Rental $15.00
Producer: Wan-Go Weng for China Institute of America
Series: Chinese History (Film 6)
Distributor: Indiana University

This film, part of the Chinese History Series, depicts the foundation of the Sui dynasty (581-618) and continues through the T'ang dynasty up to the An Lu Shan rebellion in 755. It is exclusively concerned with historical rather than religious material. The colorful Empress Wu is mentioned along with her patronage of Budhism and some shots of the great Buddha Vairocana at Lung Men. The union of the Three Teachings Buddhism, Confucianism, and Taoism—is mentioned as the ideological backbone of this properous age. Exquisite works of gold, silver, and ceramic are displayed effectively. The photography is brilliant throughout as porcelain, printing, and casting techniques are catalogued. Finally, the court of Hsuan Tsung, and his love for the beautiful Yang Keui-Fei, is described, and the downfall of the T'ang ensues with the rebellious general An Lu Shan.

This film offers a very attractive display of the rich art works of the period, effectively combining tasteful selection, cinematic technique, and narrative context.

China: The Great Cultural Mix (A.D. 220 to A.D. 581)
  17 minutes, color, 16mm, 1977
  Sale $280.00, Rental $15.00
  Videocassette
  Sale $196.00
  Producer: Wan-Go Weng for China Institute of Ameica
  Distributor: Indiana University
  Series: Chinese History

This film tells the history of China from the fall of the later Han and
the rise of the three kingdoms, Wei, Shu, Han (220-280), to the
Northern Wei (386-539). It uses a mixture of landscapes and works of
art to tell the story of China's political disorder and openness to foreign
influences, especially Buddhism, and it recounts the travels of the
Chinese pilgrims to India, such as Fa Hsien. It then backtracks to
briefly recount the stories of the Buddha and Confucius, although it
makes the misleading point that Buddha was basically "other-
worldly" and Confucius basically "this worldly."

While cinematically creative and often quite beautiful in its effects,
the almost exclusive use of artworks limits the usefulness this film to
the study of Chinese art. For Chinese history, see *The Ancient Chinese*,
and for Buddhism, Wan-Go Weng's later *Buddhism in China*.

China: The Heavenly Khan (A.D. 618 to A.D. 907)
  22 minutes, color, 16mm, 1977
  Sale $280.00, Rental $15.00
  Videocassette
  Sale $196.00
  Director/Producer: Wan-Go Weng for Chinese Institute of America
  Series: Chinese History
  Distributor: Indiana University

This film treats in considerable detail the glorious cultural expan-
sion of the T'ang, focusing on its influence in Central Asia, Korea, and
Japan. Contacts with the Arabs and Persians are discussed, as well as
the pluralistic tolerance of Islam, Nestorianism, and Manicheism. The
film properly emphasizes the great importance of Buddhism during
these times, both as a dominant ideology and as a vehicle of cross-
cultural linkage and transmission, and the formation of the Chinese
schools of Pure Land and Ch'an. It also discusses the spread of
Buddhism and Chinese culture to Japan. Prince Shotoku, Ganjin, and
Kukai are among the figures mentioned in this section, and there is
some excellent footage taken in Japan, showing how in monuments
such as the Todaiji the architectural style and grandeur of the T'ang is
still preserved.

In two respects, this film is stronger than the other films in this series. The area covered is more focused and utilizes actual monuments and landscapes of Japan instead of relying exclusively on works of art.

Chinese Legends, Gods and Prophets
  9 minutes, 16mm, 1973
  Sale $150.00, Rental $15.00
  Director/Producer: Sumner Glimcher
  Writer: Joan Glimcher
  Distributor: International Film Foundation, Inc.
  Also available from: UCt

This film ranges over the variety of Chinese religion touching on Confucianism, Taoism, and Buddhism, using artworks and monuments along with scenes of modern religious life from Taiwan and Hong Kong. It focuses in particular on the colorful festival of the sea-goddess Matsui, showing in an interesting way the syncretic mix between Confucianist, Taoist, Buddhist, and folk elements. It is relatively free of stereotypes and chauvinistic bias; it mentions, for example, how Confucius set forth the "Golden Rule" five centuries before Christ.

This film might be useful for a course on Chinese religion or history to show something of the realities of Chinese popular ritual. It shows some colorful scenes of people and places which convey the flavor of Chinese life and culture. By itself, however, it would be of little use for the study of Buddhism. The slide set *Chinese Religions* provides a more substantial introduction to contemporary Chinese religious practices.

Chinese Sculpture Through the Ages
  20 minutes, b/w, 16mm, 1965
  Sale $185.00, Rental $7.70
  Director: Wan-Go Weng
  Producer: China Film Enterprises of America
  Distributor: Pictura Film Distribution Corp.
  Also available from: UAriz, UCB, IndU, UIowa, UMich, PennSt

This film attempts to convey the richness of Chinese sculpture from the Shang Dynasty to recent times. While some of the objects are fine specimens of their kind, it is difficult to appreciate them in such an overcrowded array. The narration provides only superficial information, even mispronouncing a number of important terms.

This film is of little or no use for the study of Buddhism, Chinese religion, art, or culture.

Journey Into the Night: Chinese Funeral Rites
   18 minutes, color, 16mm, 1976
   Sale $200.00, Rental $25.00
   Producer: Gary Seaman
   Series: Chinese Cult of the Dead (Part II)
   Distributor: Far Eastern Audio Visual

This film provides a colorful and informative account of a Chinese funeral conducted in Taiwan by a large extended family and group of friends, assisted by a troupe of hired ritual actors who impersonate Buddhist and Confucian priests. An outdoor temple is erected with screens and hanging scroll paintings, with images of the Buddha Amitabha on one side and numerous lurid representations of the halls of hell on the other. Preparation of the soul tablets—red for the ancestors and white for the deceased—is depicted. There is a remarkable description of the bureaucracy of hell where clerks consult immaculate records of the soul's merit and demerit, and appropriate fees and fines are determined, to be paid by the surviving relatives during ritual performances. The Buddhist syncretism with Confucian filial piety and Taoist folk elements is interestingly conveyed in this remarkable ritual.

This is a useful film for bringing to life the realities of folk religious rituals, as well as illustrating the way in which Buddhist doctrines of karma and the cosmology of hell and the future life are understood on the popular level of Chinese culture.

Slides

Chinese Religions
   180 slides, n.d., color
   Sale $65.00, Rental $15.00
   Text: James H. Ware, Jr.
   Editor: Charles A. Kennedy
   Series: Asian Religions Media Resources
   Distributor: Visual Educational Services, Yale Divinity School

To a greater extent than other sets in the Yale series, this set of slides concentrates on religious practice. Almost all the slides are from Taiwan and Hong Kong. Neither the slides nor the accompanying essay treats the history of Buddhism in mainland China. Before the main section in Buddhism (91-167), the involvement of Buddhism in such popular practices as funeral rites (1-21), divination (22-52), and Chinese folk religion are developed. The Buddhism section focuses on monastic and temple practices. Slides 107-114 show a week-long sutra reading, and slides 119-136 cover some of the main events of an ordination ceremony. Sha Tin (The Temple of Ten Thousand

Buddhas) in Hong Kong is shown in some detail (138-151), as is Castle Peak Monastery (153-162). The text takes pains to show that there is a degree to eclecticism in the shrines, with Taoist and folk deities influencing Chinese Buddhism.

Recordings

Chinese Buddhist Music
  Recording by John Levy
  Notes by Laurence Pickens and John Levy
  Lyrichord Records (LLST 7222)

This record includes selections from a number of temples in Hong Kong and Taiwan. The bands on side one are identified as "Waking the Monks;" "From Morning Service;" "Reciting the Names of the Buddha, with Large Bell;" "Fan Pai, Solo Chant, Two hymns," "From Morning Service, Nuns (Dragon Mountain Temple, Taipei)," "From the Great Bear Liturgy (Good Fortune Temple)." On side two are band one, "Fan Pai, Solo Chant, from the Hua Yen Tsumu Liturgy (Bamboo Grove Meditation Temple);" bands 2 and 3, "From Plenary Requiem Mass;" bands 4 (a & b) "From Annual Ceremony at the Graves of Ancestors;" and bands 5, 6, and 7, "Private Requiem Mass."

The notes claim that the average Chinese finds the hymns largely unintelligible without seeing the text, and the authors are content to leave the Western listener equally uninformed. As this is the only record of Chinese Buddhist music now available, this is especially unfortunate. Those who have the slide set *Chinese Religions* might find this record a useful supplement. Lyrichord has a companion album on Taoist music, as well as a number of recordings of Chinese Art music.

CHAPTER 6

Japan and Korea

Films

Art and Spirit
Arts of Japan: Bridge of Beauty
The Buddha*
Buddhism and Shintoism in Japan
Buddhism: Land of the Disappearing Buddha—Japan*
Buddhist Art*
Buddhist Dances of Korea
Gen: Mystery of Mysteries
The Gods of Japan
Haiku
Haiku: An Introduction to Poetry
Hiraizumi: Capital of the North
Honorable Mountain
Horyuji Temple
Japan: Land of the Kami
Japan: The Living Tradition—"Religious Experience" (Part I)
Japan: The Living Tradition—"Religious Experience" (Part II)
Japanese Calligraphy
Jizo Children's Festival
Kyudo: Japanese Ceremonial Archery
Nara and Kyoto: The Cultural Heritage of Japan
Nara, Japan
Noh Drama
The Path
Pulguk-sa Temple
Religions of Korea
Restoration of the Golden Shrine
Ryokan: The Poet Priest
Smiling Images of the Buddha
The Spider's Thread
Spirit of Zen
Torches of Todaiji
Woodblock Mandala: The World of Shiko Munakata
Yakushiji Temple: The Cream of the Buddhist Arts
Zen Facets of Japanese Religion
Zen in Life*
Zen in Ryoko-in*
Zen Training of Young Monk

Slides

The Arts of Japan
Buddhism in Japan
The Buddhist Tradition: Buddhism in Japan*
Japan: Ancient Buddhist Paintings
Japan—Shinto and Buddhism
Japanese Gardens
Korean Religion
Nara and Kyoto
Philosophy of Zen
Zen

Recordings

A Bell Ringing in the Empty Sky
Buddhist Chant
Buddhist Drums, Bells and Chants
Japanese Buddhist Ritual
Music of Japan IV: Buddhist Music
Shomyo—Buddhist Ritual from Japan
The Way of Eheiji

Films

Art and Spirit
  28 minutes, color, 16mm, n.d.
  Director: Frederick Frank
  Producer: Omoto Foundation
  Distributor: Frederick Frank

Although it appears at the outset to be a general introduction to Omoto, one of the "new religions" of Japan, this film is primarily concerned with Omoto's interest in aesthetic experiences and artistic expression. Omoto is perhaps more generally eclectic and specifically Shinto than it is Buddhist, but the film emphasizes its relation to the traditional Buddhist-influenced arts such as painting, pottery, wabi tea, and Noh drama. The interpretation of these arts, moreover, uses characteristic Buddhist notions such as the centrality of tranquil silence in the tea ceremony as the manifestation of the "Pure Land" on earth.

For those interested in the Buddhist-influenced traditional arts of Japan, or in a religion focusing on the aesthetic, or in the process by which Buddhist forms and expressions influence a more syncretistic religious movement, this film might be useful. However, for its effective use, additional explanation and discussion would be needed, perhaps additional reading on the Omoto religion. More complete treatment of these arts can be found in films devoted to each of these particular arts (see Index).

*Reviewed in Section I: General and Historical Introductions

Arts of Japan: Bridge of Beauty
    29 minutes, b/w, 16mm, 1954
    Out of print
    Producer: U.S. Office of Education
    Also available from: UMich, UMinn, PennSt, UWash

This film briefly shows various traditional arts of Japan, both in their classical and more contemporary modes, through the eyes of an American artist who is in search of the underlying meaning of these arts as a "bridge of beauty" between East and West. The arts represented are Noh drama, gardens, tea ceremony, Kabuki, wood-block painting, pottery, and sumi (ink) painting.

The film is a relatively old but sensitive treatment of these arts, and shows an implicit awareness of their religious or spiritual under-pinnings—particularly concerning their relation to "emptiness" and to meditative experience. Since this awareness is not made explicit, however, this film would be useful for Buddhist studies only if accompanied by the guidance of a teacher or readings; for example, Hisamatsu's *Zen and the Fine Arts*. In addition, films focusing on each of these arts might be usefully shown (see Index).

Buddhism and Shintoism in Japan
    16 minutes, color, 16mm, 1968 (reissue)
    Sale $240.00, Rental $24.00 Study Guide included
    Director/Producer: Lew Ayers
    Series: Altars of the World
    Distributor: Threshold Films
    Also available from: BU

Accompanied by narrator and guide Lew Ayers, this film attempts—as the "Teacher's Study Guide" states—"an overview of the range of Buddhist and Shinto religious practices in Japan and their impact on Japanese culture." Aside from the treatment of Shinto, which the film in no way relates to Buddhism in Japan, we in fact find a rather superficial and misleading sampling of selected Buddhist practices and teachings in mid-twentieth-century Japan. At best, the film suggests something of the nature and practice of Buddhism in the variety of its levels and kinds, with particular reference to folk practices and cultural influences, and the sects of the True Pure Land ("Shin") and Zen. At worst, it perpetuates stereotypes and misunder-standings of Buddhism generally, Zen particularly, and their relations to Japanese culture.

This film can be recommended for use only if accompanied by careful qualification and guidance—something not provided, inci-dentally, in the "Teacher's Study Guide." Better films exist as general introductions to contemporary Japanese Buddhism; for example, *Buddhism: Land of the Disappearing Buddha—Japan* and other films in this section on Buddhism in Japan.

Buddhist Dances of Korea
  18 minutes, color, 16mm, 1969
  Sale $225.00, Rental $10.00
  Producer: University of Washington Archives of Ethnic Music and
    Dance
  Series: Ethnic Music and Dance (Robert Garfies, editor)
  Distributor: University of Washington

In this film, three dances with musical accompaniment and one instrumental piece are performed, without narration or explanation. The dances include "Na Bi Ch'um" (Butterfly Dance), "Pop Go Ch'um" (Monk's Dance), and "Ch'onsu Para" (Cymbal Dance). The instrumental piece is "Tae Ch'wi Ta" (Royal Procession Music).

Although the film has no narration and offers no explanation, these dances appear to be performances done by monks on festival occasions, and thereby represent a Korean Buddhist form of ritual dance and music. However, the film would need additional commentary and information to be useful for the study of Buddhism. Even then, it is narrowly limited in what it illustrates, and does not have the breadth of coverage that the title implies.

Gen: Mystery of Mysteries
  33 minutes, b/w, 16mm, 1973
  Sale $145.00, Rental preview only
  Producer: Kanatsu Shunji for NHK-TV
  Distributor: Japan Society

This imaginative film seeks to express the feeling of *gen* a term in Japanese (and Chinese) thought suggesting that which lies beyond and/or hidden in the form of things—the dark mystery, sublime silence, or formless form of things (compare Japanese-Buddhist aesthetic term 'yugen'). With no narration, but an interesting musical soundtrack and an effective use or black-and-white photography, the film succeeds in suggesting the dark, mysterious, ineffable character of a "reality" which is both in—yet somehow beyond—the transitory world of everyday form and experience. A veritable collage of visual forms is offered, from grey natural scenes juxtaposed with human movement and calligraphy to recurring images of the moon and meditation.

While some might not consider *gen* as Buddhist—or, indeed, religious—the film makes the unspoken connection to Buddhism in its final sequences on Zen meditation and the Zen calligraphic circle symbolizing Emptiness. In this light, the film seems to be suggesting that *gen* finally points to the Emptiness of all form, yet form as Emptiness too.

Like other films that are suggestive and implicit in character, such as *The Path*, this one would need some introduction and discussion in drawing connections to Buddhism. In addition, it would be useful to have read material related particularly to the term 'yugen' in Japanese Buddhist culture.

The Gods of Japan
  26 minutes, color, 16mm, 1973
  Sale $415.00, Rental $28.00
  Narrator: Edward P. Morgan
  Producer: Howard Enders, ABC News
  Series: Directions
  Distributor: Xerox Films
  Also available from: USo Fla, UIowa, PennSt.

By employing a general historical framework for its presentation, this film attempts a survey of religion in Japan. Particular attention is given to traditional and more contemporary forms of Shinto; to the Buddism of the Nichiren, Pure Land and Zen sects; to folk practices showing the interplay of Shinto and Buddhism; and to the new religions of Tenrikyo and Soka Gakkai.

While this film can be applauded for its attempt to present Japanese religion generally, and Buddhism specifically, as actually lived (and has interesting footage reflecting this), it is in varying degrees marred by the perpetuation of cultural and religious stereotypes, erroneous and misleading interpretations, and unsympathetic, insensitive—even inflammatory—treatments of Nichiren Buddhism and State Shinto. Narrated in a wooden fashion, the film suggests some of the following half-truths: Buddhism in Japan can be generally subsumed under the "gods of Japan," and Buddha may be understood as "God" who manifests himself in a variety of forms; Nichiren Buddhism was warlike and fanatical; popular religion is best understood as magical, miraculous and reward-granting ritual; Japanese religion has a "harmonious" future ahead of it.

This film should be used only with caution and qualification. While perhaps useful for some of its footage on popular religions and Buddhism in Japan, it is not as good as *Japan: The Living Tradition—Religious Experience (Parts I & II)* on Japanese religion generally or *Buddhism: Land of the Disappearing Buddha—Japan* on Japanese Buddhism specifically.

Haiku
  18 minutes, color, 16mm, 1974
  Sale $305.00
  Director: Andrew Welsh
  Producer: Sincinkin for Ontario Educational Communications
    Authority

Distributor: ACI, c/o Paramount Communications
Also availble from: UIll, Purdue, UMinn, SyrU, KentSt

This film focuses on traditional Japanese haiku as represented in the poetry of Basho (1644-1694), Buson (1715-1783), and Issa (1763-1827). Against a background of traditional Japanese music, and visuals generally representative of the narrative content, the film seeks to get at the underlying meaning of haiku poetry, and to provide examples of that poetry from the three poets listed above. The connection of haiku to Buddhism (Zen) is explicitly mentioned in reference to Basho, and implicitly expressed in the characterization of haiku as "capturing the limitless eternal, and the absolute tranquility of this present moment."

Although marred by an occasionally obtrusive musical background, sometimes overly contrived scenes, and poetry read with a thick Japanese accent, this is perhaps the best film on haiku as a Buddhist-influenced art form in Japan. More explicitly and clearly done than *Haiku: An Introduction to Poetry,* this film might well be used in conjunction with studies of Buddhism and the arts in Japan, and with such films as *Noh Drama, Japanese Calligraphy, Kyudo: Ceremonial Archery of Japan,* and *The Path.*

Haiku: An Introduction to Poetry
11 minutes, color, 16mm, 1970
Sale $176.00, Rental preview only
Producer: Illinois Institute of Design for Coronet Instructional
Films
Distributor: Coronet Instructional Films
Also available from: UCol, UCt, FlaSt, Boise, UIll, IndU, BU, UMich, SyrU, KentSt, UWisc

Through attractive visuals of natural scenes and an appealing musical sound track, this film suggests haiku as the poetic expression of the direct experience of the natural world. Although no explicit reference is made to Buddhist influence or content, the film does imply the Japanese background and the Buddhist content by such comments as: "In haiku I am the sunrise, the water, the bird;" or, "When the word and the object are one, that is haiku." In addition, it seems to paraphrase the great haiku master Basho when the narrator suggests that "one loses one's self in the moment of awareness and everything turns into haiku."

This film would be difficult to use without appropriate explanation of the relation between haiku and Buddhism in Japan. It would also be impossible to use for examples of actual poems since while there may well be haiku in the verbal content of the film, they are never identified as such and one is left guessing if the poetic words one just heard were, in fact, a haiku. Readings in Basho, or in Zen and its relation to haiku, would be well advised. See, for examples, books on haiku by R. H. Blyth.

This film might be related to other films concerned with the traditional arts of Japan, especially sumi painting, calligraphy, archery, and tea ceremony.

Hiraizumi: Capital of the North
   30 minutes, 16mm, 1973
   Sale $170.00 color; $110.00, b/w, $88.00, ¾" videocassette, Rental preview only
   Director: Matsudai
   Producer: NHK Japan Broadcasting Company
   Distributor: Japan Society, Inc.
   Also available from: UMich

Although ostensibly focusing on a city (Hiraizumi) and its temple (Chusonji), dedicated to preserving its twelfth century Fujiwara connections and traditions, this film reveals a "slice of life" in a working temple/community relationship. This working relationship, in turn, reveals the integration of various religious, historic, artistic, and social factors. All these dimensions are perhaps best represented in the scenes showing rehearsal for, and performance of, the Noh play "Hiraizumi" by local priests and farmers. More specifically, this film shows something of the art and architecture of Chusonji, the nature of a married hereditary priesthood, the layman's role in supporting the temple, the rituals and performing arts important to the temple and surrounding area, and the value placed on the preservation of the distinctive traditions of the temple.

While the film might be criticized for lack of a clear theme and focused exposition, it is one of the best films to present Buddhism effectively as an integral part of community life. Further, it is excellent for indicating the importance of religion in Japan as a way of fostering and preserving traditional art forms. (see *Restoration of the Golden Shrine* for further visual material on Chusonji temple, and *Torches of Todaiji* for another example of Buddhism's relation to the performing arts).

Honorable Mountain
   22 minutes, color, 16mm, 1969
   Sale discontinued
   Director/Producer: Ray Fielding
   Distributor: Bailey Films Associates
   Also available from: UCt, SyrU

This film follows a pilgrimage up Mount Fuji, one of the several sacred mountains of Japan. While the Shinto meaing of the mountain and the pilgrimage is present, the Buddhist content is expressed through references to the Buddha, and to such Buddhist practices as "chanting to purify the six senses."

While this film is unique in presenting pilgrimage as a part of Japanese Buddhist practice, an overly dramatic narrative and sound track, and the lack of a more complete and expert explanation of the Buddhist implications of the pilgrimage, mar its quality. The lack of expertise is evidenced, for example, in referring to the Kamakura Daibutsu (Daibatsu [sic]) as "God," and to Buddha in general as the "creator of heaven and earth."

Horyuji Temple
   22 minutes, color, 16mm, n.d.
   Sale Japan only (inquire from distributor)
   Producer/Distributor: Iwanami Productions
   Also available from: IowaSt

The visual content of this film includes an overview of this famous eighth century temple in Nara, a closer look at three of its major buildings (the pagoda, main hall, and "dream" hall), and some of the major art treasures located therein (the Shakyamuni triad, the famous Kudara and Yumechigai Kannons, and the bas-reliefs showing Buddha's death). In the process, brief attempts are made to depict the life of the Buddha and the meaning of Buddhism.

While this film is valuable for representing Buddhist sculpture of early Japan, it is flawed by its occasionally misleading narration, and by an overdramatic, distracting sound track. Moreover, it does not discuss the significance of the temple or its art, but tends merely to identify it. Complementary films on early Japanese iconography and architecture are *Yakushiji Temple . . .* and *Buddhist Art* (reviewed in Section I).

Japan: Land of the Kami
   27 minutes, color, 16mm, 1963
   Sale $300.00, Rental none
   Producer: Bach-Horizon
   Distributor: Sterling Educational Films
   Also available from: IndU, UIowa, SyrU, UNev, PennSt, BYU

As the title of this film suggests, Buddhism is treated in the larger context of Japanese religion generally and Shinto specifically. The focus is on religion and/or Buddhism in post-World War II Japan, with a particular concern for "new religions" such as Tenrikyo, "Messianity," Konkokyo, and Risshokoseikai. The film includes sequences suggestive of traditional Shinto and Buddhism (Zen, Tendai), but is predominantly interested in showing religious revival in contemporary Japan. Sequences on a Shinto and a Risshokoseikai festival, and on the sacred dance and music of Shinto, are also shown.

Despite its useful footage on the new religions and Shinto, the film occasionally confuses Buddhism with Shinto and interprets Japanese religion in Christian categories such as "worship" and "God." For example, Zen satori is characterized as "divine realization." The narrative content by Marcus Bach concludes with general comments about mankind's spiritual needs, and declares that worship is the joy supreme" and "Japan is the land of Gods."

Japan: The Living Tradition—"Religious Experience" (Part I)
30 minutes, color, videocassette, 1976
Sale $225.00
Director: E.O. Reischauer and Jackson Bailey
Producer: University of Mid-America
Series: Japan: The Living Tradition
Distributor: University of Mid-America (sale only)

This presentation attempts to identify a core of what constitutes religious experience in contemporary Japan. This core is identified as a special relationship to nature, reverence for special objects and people, identity and "safe passage through life," education and right action. Expressions of this core are various, and Buddhist elements play their part—most explicitly in rites of passage connected with death and ancestral spirits, and less explicitly in austerity training.

This presentation admirably attempts to go beyond stereotyped Western notions of the meaning of religion for the Japanese, and suggests that the religious dimension of human existence is woven seamlessly into the fabric of daily life. Beyond that, however, it not only has minimal explicitly Buddhist content but suffers at key points on both substantive and stylistic grounds. Specifically, it remains unsophisticated and unclear regarding criteria for determining something as religious, and presents what at times is a confusing picture of just what might be included under this category for the Japanese. Stylistically, the presentation seems to wander from the main theme too easily, and resorts to still photography and an inappropriate musical sound track to carry its message.

While designed as the first of two segments on religion in a complete video course on Japan, this segment can stand by itself as a distinct and self-contained presentation. However, as an introduction to Buddhism in contemporary Japan, a film like *Buddhism: Land of the Disappearing Buddha—Japan* is superior.

Japan: The Living Tradition—"Religious Experience" (Part II)
  30 minutes, color, videocassette, 1976
  Sale $225.00
  Director: E.O. Reischauer and Jackson Bailey
  Producer: University of Mid-America
  Series: Japan: The Living Tradition
  Distributor: University of Mid-America (sale only)

In contrast to Part I of this two-part series on "Religious Experience," this film presents a general and historical overview of the major religious traditions in Japan, with special reference to Shinto, Buddhism, Confucianism, and Christianity. The segments on Buddhism deal primarily with the coming of Buddhism in the sixth century and its relation to the state; basic doctrines; the major sects of Tendai, Pure Land, Nichiren, and Zen; and contemporary urban forms of Buddhism such as Soka Gakkai.

This presentation could well function as a general survey of Japanese religious history, and of sectarian Buddhism within that history. Unfortunately, however, it suffers from the general malady of such surveys in its tendency to offer cliches and caricatures of its subject. These factors are not aided by the superimposed music which is at times inappropriate to the nature of the visual material.

Part II of this two-part series can well stand independently of Part I. Indeed, no attempt is made in either part to relate one to the other. This can be of value, of course, but it is important to bear in mind and confusion resulting from the conflicting conceptions of religion presented in the two parts, and the degree to which they remain unintegrated in this program.

Japanese Calligraphy
  15 minutes, b/w, 16mm, 1957
  Sale $125.00, Rental $12.50
  Producer: Pierre Alechinsky
  Distributor: Audio Brandon Films
  Also available from: UNev, SyrU, PennSt, UWash

While no explicit reference is made to Buddhist influences or content, this film focuses on an important art form in Japan which has been influenced by Buddhism—namely, shodo, the "Way of the Brush." Sequences include the training in a child's early education, and the accomplished calligraphy of masters exemplary of both traditional and more avant-garde modes. In the process, the relation of calligraphy to painting is made clear, the importance of discipline and training leading to freedom and spontaneity is stressed, and the tension between traditional and avant-garde forms is indicated. Various comments in the film suggest the Buddhist connections such as, "Do not write with your hand or your arm, write with your heart (mind)" or, "one moves from meditation to creation."

This mid-twentieth century French film makes perhaps too much of a kind of anti-establishment, existentialist avant-garde in calligraphy, and not enough of the traditional religious influences. However, it might well be useful as an example of Buddhist influences on the traditional arts of Japan when accompanied with appropriate readings or lectures.

The film might relate well to other films dealing with the traditional arts of Japan, especially those concerned with sumi painting, archery, haiku poetry, and tea ceremony.

Jizo Children's Festival
   30 minutes, color, 16mm, 1973
   Sale $205.00, Rental preview only
   Producer: NHK Japan Broadcasting Company
   Distributor: Japan Society Inc.
   Also available from: UMich

This film takes the viewer through major aspects of the celebration of Jizo Bon in Kyoto—a children's festival honoring the Bodhisattva Jizo (Skt. Kshitigarbha) who, in Japan, is a guardian spirit for the souls of dead children. It makes clear clear the community and family involvement in a festival whose intent—as far as the film is concerned—is largely the entertainment of the children. There are also extended sequences showing the art of silk cloth weaving in the particular district of Kyoto chosen for the film's location.

The film is colorful and generally entertaining, and it might appeal especially to younger viewers interested in the religious festivals and customs of other lands. For more mature educational purposes, it generally underemphasizes any religious significance and historical background for this festival, and overemphasizes its entertaining, secular character. In spite of this failing, the film describes the nature and preservation of such festivals in the contemporary urban setting, and the importance of lay and/or popular Buddhism in Japan.

Kyudo: Japanese Ceremonial Archery
   10 minutes, color, 16mm, 1970
   Sale $175.00
   Producer: ACI, c/o Paramount Communications
   Distributor: University of Illinois Audio Visual Services
   Also available from: Boise, UIll, SyrU

This film provides a brief look at the training, style, and ideals of kyudo or the "Way of the Bow." About half of the footage shows the shooting style from a standing position, while the rest shows shooting from running horseback called yabusami. By focusing on the Ogusuwara school of archery this film shows the importance of disciplined training, form and tradition, proper breathing and concentration, and calming the mind. The goal of such archery is said to be "perfect style" rather than hitting the target.

Although too brief, and marred by a rather abrupt ending, the film successfully depicts kyudo. Unfortunately, it makes no explicit reference to Buddhist or other religious influences on archery specifically or the martial arts generally. It does not even explicate the meaning of "ceremonial" in the title. The only religious connection is suggested by sequences of yabusami at a Shinto shrine in Nikko. The film would be useful, therefore, only with supporting information and interpretation concerning the relation of contemporary kyudo to Zen Buddhism provided by such readings at Herrigel's *Zen and the Art of Archery* which would provide the necessary context for the Buddhist interpretation of such a characteristic comment as: "When the man, the bow, and the arrow are one, the arrow is released."

This film might well be related to other films dealing with the traditional arts of Japan, especially sumi painting, calligraphy, haiku poetry, and tea ceremony.

Nara and Kyoto: The Cultural Heritage of Japan
   45 minutes, color, 16mm, ca., 1960
   Out of print
   Producer: Kiroku Eigasha Productions
   Distributors: Inquire, Japan Society, Inc.

As its title suggests, the explicit theme of this film is the cultural heritage of Japan as seen though the prominent art and architecture of Nara and Kyoto. The relevance lies both in the degree to which Buddhism has been a part of that heritage, and in the degree to which the film focuses almost exclusively on Buddhist elements of that heritage. More specifically, the film surveys in very summary fashion the major temples and Buddhist arts of Nara, and most of the obvious highlights of Buddhist and non-Buddhist Kyoto culture up into the Tokugawa Period.

The film includes some excellent photography and a visual sweep of Buddhist-inspired Japan. But it suffers from a superficial and cliched approach to its topic. By neglect of other aspects it over-emphasizes Buddhism in Japan's religious pluralism. These faults, together with a stilted narrative style, an over-dramatic sound track, and the poor quality of the print reviewed, limits this film's utility for academic study.

Nara, Japan
   21 minutes, color, 16mm, 1968
   Sale Japan only, Rental free
   Producer: Shin Nippon Productions for Nara Perfecture
   Distributor: Japan Foundation
   Also available from: IowaSt

In the framework of a general survey of Nara's traditional culture, this film gives Buddhism prominent coverage. Included are brief views of Horyuji, Yakushiji, and Todaiji temples—together with their main art treasures—and a sequence showing the training of Shugendo priests on Mount Yoshino.

The strength of this film lies in the brief but clear presentation of key sculpted figures, and footage on the training of Shugendo priests. However, the narration often fails to provide adequate explanation of this material. This is particularly true in the sequence on the Shugendo sect which is not only unidentified but is presented as something "strange." There is better coverage of Nara art and architecture in such films as *Yakushiji Temple . . .* or *Horyuji Temple.*

Noh Drama
   30 minutes, color, 16mm, 1965
   Sale Japan only*, Rental free
   Producer: Sakura Motion Picture Company for the Japanese Ministry of Foreign Affairs
   Distributor: Japan Foundation
   Also available from: UCol, BYU, UWisc
   *To purchase, contact the producer (listed in appendix of distributors).

There is little in this film to suggest the important connections between Noh and Buddhism. However, excerpts from several plays are shown with an occasional hint of the Buddhist influences on the plot content, as for example, a Buddhist exorcism sequence. Plays excerpted are: "Fujito," "Shojo," "Takasago," "Tsuchigumo," "Dojoji" and in more extended form, "Matsukaze." Performances are by the Hosso and Kanze schools of Noh.

This film would be useful *only* in a specialized context of study where the complete plays were read and additional information provided concerning the influence of Buddhism on both the content and the performance ideals of the plays. For other films illustrating Noh, see the Index. For an interesting and complementary view of Kabuki, see *Torches of Todaiji.*

The Path
  33 minutes, color, 16mm, 1976
  Sale $345.00, Rental $35.00
  Director: John Adair and David Hilberman
  Produce: Sumai Films
  Distributor: University of Illinois Audio Visual Services
  Also available from: UCB, PennSt, USoCar

This imaginative and well-executed film provides a detailed look at a tea ceremony in the Omoto Senkei style with occasional relevant sayings suggestive of the underlying principles of the Way of Tea. While Buddhism is never mentioned, these sayings make relatively clear the Buddhist and Zen influences on the Japanese tea ceremony. For example, it is indicated that "the path of tea is the path of everyday life—a path both ancient and yet in the mindless Void;" or, "a path beyond subject/object distinctions out of which actions might flow effortlessly."

These sayings are occasional, however, and the overall impression of the film is silence within an aesthetic environment punctuated only by the sounds of water and people making or drinking tea. This silence is at once the strength and the potential weakness of the film. On the one hand, it expresses and draws one into the wordless presence of tea, but on the other hand, it risks incurring tedium and misunderstanding with its extended unaccompanied visuals and lack of explanation. No doubt the silence is intended—not only to invite the viewer's participation, but to exemplify tea's wordlessness and "purposelessness." ("What is the purpose of tea? Why trouble to ask?" says the narrator.) However, some viewers might not readily identify with this ritual and be left fundamentally outside the film.

The usefulness of this film depends in large degree on background reading and explanation. With proper preparation, it becomes uniquely excellent as an introduction to the tea ceremony, and might well be used in conjunction with other films concerned with the Buddhist or Zen influenced arts; for example, *Arts of Japan: Bridge of Beauty, Japanese Calligraphy, Noh Drama, Haiku,* or *Ken in Ryoko-in* (see Section I).

A detailed guide has been prepared to accompany this film, but does not come with rental. Entitled, "Japanese Tea: The Ritual, The Aesthetics, The Way," it is available for purchase from MSS Information Corporation (655 Madison Avenue, New York, NY 10021).

Pulguk-sa Temple
  22 minutes, color, 16mm, n.d.
  Sale none, Rental free
  Producer: Korean Film Board
  Distributor: Korean Consulate

This film depicts the recently restored fifth century temple of the Silla Kingdom. It presents the temple as a store house of numbered "national treasures," including a stone-by-stone view of the main hall and views of the various bridges, stone pagodas, and portels. The film concludes with footage of the Sukullum Cave Temple, showing low-bas sculpture on the cave walls and a beautiful monolithic statue of Sakhyamuni.

Although interesting from an art-historical point of view, and for its view of Pulguk-sa Temple as an important indicator of Korean national pride, this film is of little use for the study of Korean Buddhism.

Some of the same material in the film is also included in *Kyongju* (Korean National Film Center), a film treatment of the capital of the Silla Dynasty.

Religions of Korea
  20 minutes, color, 16mm, n.d.
  Sale none, Rental free
  Producer: Korean Film Productions
  Distributor: Korean Consulate

This film begins with a brief treatment of ancient Korean Shamanism and then proceeds to a brief account of the introduction of Buddhism to Korea. Through stills and artwork the film shows Korean monks defending their country against foreign invasion at the end of the nineteenth century, and similarly points to the patriotic function of organized religion throughout Korean history.

The film proceeds from a treatment of Buddhism to other religious traditions including Confucianism, Islam, and various Christian sects.

Restoration of the Golden Shrine
  50 minutes, color, 16mm, n.d.
  Sale $360.00, Rental preview only.
  Producer: NHK Japan Broadcasting Company
  Distributor: Japan Society, Inc.
  (English version or script is reportedly available with purchase)

This film offers a highly detailed look a the arts and architecture of the Buddhist temple of Chusonji near the city of Hiraizumi in Japan, and at the process of the recently completed restoration. Without English narration or script, as in the copy used for this review, this film would not be very useful except for its visual content. To see Chusonji in another light and another context, see *Hiraizumi: Capital of the North.*

Ryokan: The Poet Priest
   27 minutes, color, 16mm, n.d.
   Sale inquire from distributor
   Producer: Matsuoka Productions
   Distributor: Orient Films Association

This film depicts the life and literary work of Ryokan (1757-1831), an (unaffiliated) Zen monk/poet known for his simplicity, humanity, and love of children and nature. The film shows scenes from the area in which he lived, monuments in his honor, paintings of him as well as his calligraphy/poetry, and portrays the recluse monk/poet ideal in traditional Japan.

This film would be most useful as supplementary material for a larger concern with Ryokan and/or Buddhist-influenced poetry and lifestyle. By itself, the film tends to focus more on Ryokan's life, character, and poetry than on any of these as expressions of his Buddhism. This film would be well complemented by films focusing on poetry (haiku) or on the relation of Zen to the arts, for example, *Zen in Ryoko-in*. (Another film on Ryokan, available only in Japan, is *In Quest of Japanese Thoughts: Ryokan's Snow, Moon and Flowers*, UNIJAP.)

Smiling Images of the Buddha
   30 minutes, color, 16mm, n.d.
   Sale $205.00, Rental preview only
   Producer: NHK Japan Broadcasting Company
   Distributor: Japan Society, Inc.
   (English version or script reportedly available with purchase)

This film focuses on the comic sculptured images of Buddhas and Bodhisattvas done by the eighteenth-century folk artist Mokujiki. Juxtaposed to his work are examples of more classic iconographic style.

The print used for this review had no narration, and the statues are simply presented by themselves against a background of playful music and miscellaneous sounds. To use this film effectively, the viewer needs additional information concerning Mokujiki and his work, or an English version of the film.

The Spider's Thread
   30 minutes, b/w, 16mm, n.d.
   Sale $110.00, Rental preview only
   Director: Tokuzo Kondo
   Producer: NHK Japan Broadcasting Company
   Distributor: Japan Society

This film is a modern musical ballet-drama originally produced for television. Based on a story of the same title written by a well-known Japanese novelist, Ryunosuke Akutagawa (1892-1927), it portrays an evil man sent to hell for his misdeeds. Because he once saved a spider's life, he is given a spider's thread lowered into the depths by the compassionate Kannon. As he climbs up the thread, he discovers other people climbing out of hell after him and he selfishly tries to make them return. As a result of this self-centered thought the thread breaks and he is plunged into hell again. The ballet-drama is an excellent example of popular Buddhist notions such as karma, hell and Kannon, rendered in a comtemporary artistic form.

The dramatic development, dance renditions, and background music (which incorporates classical Japanese instruments) are all excellent. Because there is no narration, however, viewers must supply the correlations between the performance and Buddhist symbolism. Despite the lack of explicit commentary on Buddhist influence, the performance clearly renders the ideal life as one typified by compassion and serenity, while selfishness and turmoil are shown to be the worst state of existence. For more traditional Japanese dance forms depicting Buddhist motifs, see *Noh Drama* or *Torches of Todaiji* (Kabuki).

Spirit of Zen
   25 minutes, b/w, 16mm, 1959
   Out of print
   Supervisor: Kishimoto Hideo
   Producer: NHK Japan Broadcasting Company
   Distributor: Inquire, Japan Society, Inc,

After a relatively brief attempt to put Zen in an historical context and to summarize its major religious intention, the film moves to its main theme—namely, to show the relationship between Zen and a variety of Japanese aesthetic principles and artistic expressions. The aesthetic principles included are "lack of balance", "simplicity", "subtlety", and "aloofness". These principles are illustrated by the arts of the garden, tea ceremony and pottery, tea houses, and Noh drama.

While one might applaud the film's attempt to do any of the above, unfortunately it succeeds only in perpetuating the mystification of Zen and a misunderstanding of the relation of Zen to Japanese arts and aesthetics. Against a background of overdramatic music and photo-graphy, the film presents Zen as a strange, mysterious, and enigmatic phenomenon, and leaves the impression that it may be equated with the aesthetic principles dealt with. Other and more recent materials have handled most of these issues with greater clarity and intelligence; for example, the slide set *Philosophy of Zen* and films such as *The Path, Zen in Ryoko-in,* or *Gen: Mystery of Mysteries.*

Torches of Todaiji
 40 minutes, color, 16mm, 1971
 Sale $290.00 color; $190.00, b/w, Rental preview only
 Producer: NHK Japan Broadcasting Company
 Distributor: Japan Society, Inc.
 Also available from: UMich

This film depicts the process by which the shunie spring ritual at Todaiji temple in Nara inspires the creation of a contemporary Kabuki drama by the great actor Onoe Shoroku. In doing so, it shows sequences from the shunie indicating its primary meaning as purification and penance on the one hand, and renewal and fecundity on the other. Sequences from the creation, rehersal, and performance of the drama are interspersed to show the relation of ritual to the creation of a dramatic form. Shoroku himself provides the thread that connects these various parts as he finds creative inspiration in the ritual and adapts it to the conventions of his art.

The film is thoroughly enjoyable, beautifully produced, and excellent for showing the way religious practices can serve as the foundations for artistic forms. However, the film relegates the shunie to secondary importance. As a result, neither the sequence, the history, or the meaning of the ritual is made completely clear. Additional reading or commentary on the ritual would be useful prior to viewing the film in the classroom. Other complementary films related to the performing arts in Japan are: *Hiraizumi: Capital of the North, Noh Drama,* and *The Spider's Thread.*

Woodblock Mandala: The World of Shiko Munakata
 30 minutes, color, 16mm, 1973
 Sale $470.00, Rental $55.00
 Producer: NHK Japan Broadcasting Company
 Distributor: Films Incorporated

This film explores the art and person of Shiko Munakata, one of Japan's most famous living artists and a master of the woodblock print. It shows much of his art, as well as the process by which he creates it, and spends considerable time explaining both his ideas about art and creativity, and those elements of Japanese culture which inspire him. Included in the later are sequences on a Jizo hall where prayers for the souls of dead children are chanted and favorite toys are stored, as well as scenes of kite art, festival lanterns, and drumming.

While his art does not necessarily focus on Buddhist themes, it does include a signficant amount of work reflecting his interest in the Bodhisattvas Jizo and Kanzeon (Kannon). Similarly, while the film does not allow us to see his art as characteristically Buddhist art, statements such as the following seem to imply at least that possibility: "I work my print as if I were gouging out the universe, a mandala of the universe." These and other statements suggesting a Buddhist emphasis are not explained or pursued, and the impression one is left with is that as an artist or creative spirit, he is more characteristically Japanese than Buddhist.

This film would need to be used with care in the context of an interest in Buddhism, for the Buddhist connections are no more explicit than the occasional Buddhist themes in his art. On the other hand, it *does* reflect the incorporation of such themes into a contemporary and important artistic expression. In this sense, the film has interesting parallels to *Gen: Mystery of Mysteries*, *The Spider's Thread*, and *Torches of Todaiji*.

Yakushiji Temple: The Cream of the Buddhist Arts
  30 minutes, color, 16mm, 1968
  Sale $410.00, Rental $40.00
  Producer: NHK Japan Broadcasting Company
  Distributor: Films Incorporated
  Also available from: UIll

This impressive film takes a close look at the art and architecture of Yakushiji, the seventh century Japanese temple which enshrines Yakushi, the "healing Buddha." The film concentrates on the temple's three central treasures—the pagoda, the Yakushi triad, and the Sho Kannon—all three of which are given considerable attention. Also shown are other sculptured images, ground plans of earlier and later versions of the temple, the various buildings which make up the compound. Occasional sequences indicate that this remains a working temple and not just a museum. An unusual example of this is the brief sequence on a spring purification ritual making use of gagaku masks.

Despite occasionally inappropriate and distracting music, and a narration which emphasizes the artistic rather than the Buddhist meaning of this material, this is perhaps the best available film on the early Buddhist art and architecture of Japan. It would be especially useful in conjunction with studies of Buddhist iconography generally, or earlier Japanese Buddhist art and symbolism. Related films are *Buddhist Art* (see Section I) and *Horyuji Temple*.

Zen Facets of Japanese Religion
  20 minutes, b/w, 16mm, n.d.
  Rental $5.00
  Director/Producer: Ysbrand Rogge for World Alive Films
  Distributor: World Alive (out of print)
  Also available from: BU

More than half this film deals with selected non-Buddhist aspects of Japanese religion, including footage on the so-called "fighting festival" of Sinto. The Buddhist material consists of scenes from a Nichiren Buddhist purification ritual, and more extended footage covering selected aspects of life in a Zen monastery.

This older black-and-white film lacks a unified view or focus on either Zen or Japanese religion. Moreover, its treatment of Zen is too brief to warrant its title. More recent productions, such as *Zen in Life*, provide a more complete view. In addition, the film is marred by the sensationalism of the "fighting festival," and a narrative soundtrack difficult to understand. Except for the brief sequences on Nichiren Buddhism, the film is of little usefulness for the study of Buddhism in Japan.

Zen Training of a Young Monk
  16 minutes, b/w, 16mm, n.d.
  Sale: inquire from distributor
  Distributor: Iwanami Productions, Inc.

This film offers a rather detailed look at the procedures involved in gaining admittance to, and training within, a Zen monastic setting—in this case at Shogenji temple in the town of Ibuka, Gifu Prefecture. Sequences are included on admission rites, meditation, taking vows, eating, work, and other aspects of the daily life.

This older black-and-white film, which is a straightforward descriptive account with a sometimes overdramatic soundtrack, may well be superseded by newer, more easily available, English-language films such as *Zen in Life*. The film is apparently available for purchase only, the only in the Japanese-language version upon which this review is based. An English synopsis accompanies the Japanese version.

Slides

The Arts of Japan
  300 slides (15 sets), color, 1964
  Sale $30.00 per set
  Producer: Byutsu Shuppan - Sha, Tokyo

Distributor: Prothman Associates (sale only)
Explanatory text: Nama Seiraki, Tani Shinichi, and Kawakita
Michiaki. 377 pp. $15.00

This slide set is a good historical survey of Japanese visual arts from the prehistoric period through modern times; fully one-third to one-half of the slides are of Buddhist images and temples. The majority of these slides are in sets II-VII, covering the Asuka period through the Kamakura period (seventh-fourteenth centuries). The Buddhist pieces included are all extremely important examples from esthetic, historical, and iconographic points of view.

The set is accompanied by a 377-page guide, devoting approximately a page to each slide and summaries of the main features of each period covered. The guide is written by a team of eminent Japanese scholars and provides valuable information on the historical context, nuances of style, iconographic detail, and religious and cultural importance of each work. Although the slides are all clear in detail, the colors of the set reviewed appear faded.

Buddhism in Japan
  25 slides (with lecture), color, 1971
  Sale: $21.95
  Producer: Shobun Kubota
  Distributor: Scholarly Publications (formerly Sheikh Productions)
    (sale only)

By its own admission, this set only attempts to provide a "broad outline" of Japanese Buddhism. It includes an eight-page history of Japanese Buddhism, and twenty-five briefly explained slides showing Buddhist practices in a variety of sects and styles (lay and monastic), and some Buddhist symbols and images.

Because of its focus on people and practice, this set might be useful as a supplement to the Yale slide set *Japanese Religions*. It might also be used as part of a more thorough introduction to the visual aspects of Japanese Buddhism, but in terms of both quality and quantity it is insufficient to stand on its own as a visual introduction to Japanese Buddhism.

Japan: Ancient Buddhist Paintings
  30 slides, color, n.d.
  Sale $26.00 Trilingual guide
  Producer: UNESCO
  Series: UNESCO World Art Series
  Distributor: UNIPUB (Sale only)

The development of Japanese painting and the history of Buddhism in Japan are closely related. This set focuses on the major painting styles and intermingling of secular and religious motifs in Japanese painting from the seventh to twelfth centuries. The guide provides a useful reminder of the influence of Buddhism or Japanese court life. The paintings include representations of Buddhas and Bodhisattvas, mandalas, landscapes, and episodes from Buddhist lore. The art is appropriately chosen and photographed, as well as clearly identified in terms of subject and style.

Japan — Shinto and Buddhism
140 slides, color
Sale $50.00, Rental $10.00
Producer: Charles A. Kennedy
Series: Asian Religious Media Resources
Distributor: Visual Education Service Yale Divinity School

This set is divided into two parts. Part I treats Shinto religious practice. Part II, Buddhism (slides 80-140), provides an overview of the history of Japanese Buddhist sects from the introduction of Buddhism in the sixth century to the present. Virtually all of the slides in this second section are of temples, statuary, and religious objects. In contrast to the *Chinese Religions* slide set in the same series, and in marked contrast with the first seventy-nine slides on Shinto, there is no emphasis on religious practice. This set attempts to relate the slides to the original textual sources, but the effort leads to a certain glibness in treating Zen with only a brief poem. Specifically, the entire treatment of Zen consists of an eight-verse poem with each verse illustrated by slides (nos. 127-136). While this is a useful collection of visual materials for teaching about Japanese Buddhism, it neglects treatment of Buddhist religious practice, and cannot stand on its own as an introduction to Japanese Buddhism.

Japanese Gardens
150 slides (with text)
Producer: Lennox Tierney
Distributor: Kai Dib Films International

This slide set focuses on an important aspect of the religious and Buddhist arts of Japan. Its significance for Buddhism lies in its emphasis on the garden as symbol rather than decoration, and on the traditional gardens connected to temples, shrines, teahouses, and imperial villas such as Katsura.

The accompanying text only briefly describes the slides, so additional information and interpretation would need to be offered especially in relating gardens to Zen or Pure Land ideals. This slide set could be complemented by the use of *Philosophy of Zen* in the same Kai Dib series.

Korean Religion
  120 images, color, 1975
  Sale $45.00, Rental $10.00
  Preparer: James H. Ware, Jr.
  Editor: Charles H. Kennedy
  Series: Asian Religions Media Resources
  Distributor: Visual Education Service, Yale Divinity School

This set is clearly one of the best of the Yale series. The guide and slides present a clear historical overview as well as examples of comtemporary practice. While slides 43-98 treat Buddhism specifically, the set provides an integrated view of how shamanism, folk religion, and Confucianism combine with Buddhism to shape Korean religious life. Slides 62-72 give details of services for the dead as conducted at Pongwon Temple, the leading center of the Tae Gu (non-celibate) order. Slides 85-89 focus on some of the traditional life style within a monastery, and are followed by slides of Won Buddhism (a "new religion") with its own focus on a militant work ethnic. The set includes temples and images from the Silla dynasty seventh to tenth centuries), as well as modern examples of art. Images of Vairocana, Kwan yin, Amida, and Maitreya are shown, as well as an unusual close-up of the "Seven Constellations" enshrined at Pongwon temple (illustrated in slides 73-77).

Nara and Kyoto
  40 color slides, 1965
  Sale $30.00/$20.00 slides; $55.00/$40.00 slides
  Slides and Text: Joseph P. Love, S.J.
  Publisher: Bijutsu Shuppam Sha
  Distributor: Prothman Associates

This is composed of two 20-slide sets each providing well-photographed views of important examples of art and architecture from Nara and Kyoto respectively. Most of the pieces are Buddhist or Buddhist-influenced. The Nara slides include views of art and architecture from the temple complexes of Yakushiji, Horyuji, Toshodaiji, and others. The Kyoto slides focus more on Zen-influenced arts including landscape paintings, calligraphy, and architecture and views of the Moss Garden at Saihoji, the garden at Daisenn, and the stone garden at Ryoanji. The guide gives informative descriptions including a judicious blend of insights to history, art history, nuances of design, and religious significance. The comments are less scholarly in tone than the set *The Arts of Japan* and less involved in the history of Buddhism than the set *Japan—Shinto and Buddhism* but they do comprise a good basic lecture on Buddhist art in Japan as evidenced at these two major sites. An instructor might consider using these slides to accompany showing such films on specific sites as *Yakushiji Temple . . . , Horyuji, Torches of Todaiji* or, of course, *Nara and Kyoto . . .* and *Nara, Japan.*

Philosophy of Zen
   100 slides (with text), 1970
   Sale $146.25
   Producer: Lennox Tierney
   Distributor: Kai Dib Films International

This set is rather mistitled; it would more accurately be called "The Zen Gardens: Seven Principles."

Based on the seven principles of Zen art established by Hisamatsu Shin'ichi (*Zen and the Fine Arts,* Kodansha Publications), the set illustrates views of gardens with the general aesthetic ideals of Zen art listed as: asymmetry (fukinsei), simplicity (kanso), austerity (koko), naturalness (shizen), profundity (yugen), detachment (datsuzoku), and tranquility (seijaku).

The quality of the slides is excellent, but the attempt to set up specific gardens to exemplify this or that principle *separately* may be misleading. Less confusing, and more appropriate to both the gardens and the principles, would be simply to look at all the gardens as they exemplify one or more of the principles. For example, the set shows the Ryoanji rock garden under koko (austerity) but in so doing ignores the other six principles. Surely, Ryoanji exemplifies *all* the principles and should be treated as such.

The accompanying text gives little explanation of the Buddhist significance of these principles. Reading in Hisamatsu would be useful background.

Zen
   25 slides, color, 1971
   Sale $21.95 35-page guide
   Producer: Dr. Takemi Takuse
   Distributor: Scholarly Publications (formerly Sheikh Productions)

This set is easily the most useful of the Skeikh series. It consists of an introductory essay on the history, lineage, and types of Zen, followed by discussions of each slide. The first fifteen slides depict aspects of monastic life in a leading Soto Zen temple, Soji-ji. Slides 4-7 illustrate the proper method of sitting in zazen with a clear discussion of its meaning and importance. Other slides include tonsure, morning and evening rituals, accepting food, receiving alms, and mundane chores. The last ten slides illustrate the spread of Zen aesthetics outside the monastery walls. These include the to-be-expected shots of flower arranging, rock gardens, tea ceremonies, calligraphy, and brush painting. Zen ritual in lay practice is also shown. This set combined with the record album *The Way of Eheiji* can provide a valuable introduction into the practice and expression of Soto Zen.

Recordings

A Bell Ringing in the Empty Sky
Goru Yamaguchi on Shakuhachi
Producer: Peter K. Siegel
Distributor: Records (#H72025)
Nonesuch

The Japanese end-blown bamboo flute known as shakuhachi has been used for centuries by Fuke Zen monks as part of their meditative practice. When the warrior samurai were disarmed and became mendicants in the seventeenth century, they are reputed to have found the sturdy instrument a worthy cudgel as well as solace in their wanderings. This recording is of two compositions from the classic shakuhachi repertory compiled by the samurai monk, Kinko. The title piece "A Bell Ringing in the Empty Sky" is regarded today as sacred music. It can be an effective classroom tool conveying a sense of a Zen mood or attitude comprehensible to untrained ears, yet beyond ordinary spoken word.

Buddhist Chant (A Recorded Survey of Actual Temple Rituals)
Recorded by Katsumasa Takasago
10-page notes
Distributor: Lyrichord Records (#LLST-7118)

This two-record set gives a variety of styles of Japanese Buddhist chant. Side one, record one, gives three selections of Zen choral chanting recorded at the Rinzai Temple, Myoshinji. The first is an adoration of Avalokiteshvara, the second a sutra of devotion to the three jewels Buddha, Dharma, and Sangha. The final selection is a recitation of the aspiration to enlightenment. Side two of record one gives examples of Goeika—group chanting of short poems by pilgrims (usually women)—followed by a shomyo-style chant performed by Tendai (Lotus school) monks. The first side of record two includes three examples of nembutsu (repetitious chanting of praise to the Buddha[s]), and a virtuoso performance of two prayers by an unidentified Zen priest. The final side gives the morning ritual of the Shuken Shi sect, an early syncretic sect combining elements of Buddhism and Shinto. The service begins with a confessional hymn associated with Tendai, followed by the *Heart Sutra,* and concluded by a prayer for world peace. The recordings are clear; the notes are not technical and perhaps err on the side of generalities. However, they do provide translations of most of the chanted passages and compare the different purposes and style of chant among those chosen. The omission of Shingon chanting style can be partially remedied by reference to the recording *Shomyo-Buddhist Ritual from Japan* (See p. 110).

Buddhist Drums, Bells, and Chants
   Recorded with notes at actual services in the temples of Kyoto, Japan
   Distributor: Lyrichord Records (#LLST-7200)

This album comes with scant descriptive notes and a two-paragraph discussion of Buddhism. Side A includes beating of the Taiko drum used in a Zen service, a group of women from the Jodo sect chanting the *Heart Sutra,* unidentified male pilgrims singing a Goeiko (pilgrimage song), and two funeral songs. Side B includes a recording of ritual music on the shakuhachi (bamboo flute), two Shomyo songs (often compared to Gregorian chants), and the ringing of the bell in Myoshinji Temple. The selections appear to have been chosen without any clear aesthetic or pedagogical purpose. There are distracting background noises in the recording and the notes are not useful.

Japanese Buddhist Ritual
   Recorded with notes by Douglas G. Haring (1956)
   Distributor: Folkways Records (#FE-4449)

This record aims at capturing the "typical" sound of Buddhist worship. The notes take the dubious position that for the average Japanese Buddhist, one temple is the same as another. That these recordings are from Tandai liturgy recorded in Normanji Temple is deemed incidental. The performers of the chanting (the temple priest and the local congregation) are not professionals, and in this sense the music may be typical of public worship across Japan. But it is misleading to assume that the chanting on this recording is the same in ritual purpose, musical style, or metaphysical content as Nichiren,

Shingon, or Zen chanting. The notes give no information on the particular passages of the lotus sutra, Wasan Goeka, or Hymn of Mount Hiei that make up the text of the liturgy. The recording includes considerable background noise.

Music of Japan IV: Buddhist Music
   Recordings and commentary by Eta Harich-Schneider (1953)
   3-page notes
   UNESCO Collection—Musical Anthology of the Orient
   Distributor: UNIPUB

Most of the music on this recording is from the Soto Zen monastery, Eiheiji. Side one includes a brief version of the drum call to prayer, followed by a complete recording of the chanting in the twice-monthly communal penitence. Side two includes a solo Kada-style chant, "Sange" (used in public purification ceremonies), a funeral hymn and processional, and the evening signal to retire, all from Eiheiji. The remaining two bands are a recording of the "Sri Mala Simha Nada Sutra" (Lion's Roar or Queen Sri Mala) from Mount Hiei, and a passage from the "Suvarna Prabhasa Sutra" (Golden Light) accompanied by lute. Both of these are given as examples of chant used in solo meditation. All but one band were recorded in the autumn of 1953, but the technical quality of the recording is good and generally free of extraneous sound. The three pages of notes give an outline of the Japanese Buddhist art of Shomyo (radiant voice) chanting, with basic classifications of scale and tempo examples of melodic notation and descriptive information on the instruments. The notes to each band include translations of the passages sung and description of their place in liturgy.

Shomyo-Buddhist Ritual from Japan (Dai Hannya ceremony, Shingon sect)
   Notes by Pierre Landy and Toshiro Kido
   Recorded by the Westdeutcher Rundfunk
   UNESCO—Musical Sources: Ceremonial Ritual and Magic Music II-3
   Distributor: UNIPIB (Phillips # 6586-021)

This record is based on a Western tour of chanters from the Buzan division of the Shingon sect. The ritual is a ceremony connected with the largely symbolic reading of the six-hundred-volume *Dai Hannya* scriptures. The Shingon or esoteric sect employs chant in similar fashion to the Tantric Buddhist schools of Tibet, and this recording may offer a comparison with Tibetan as well as with other schools of Japanese Buddhism.

The notes give some indication of the teaching of chant and its transmission from master to student over the generations. However, there is neither detail given about the different stages of the ceremony recorded nor any translation of what is being chanted.

The Way of Eheiji
   Recording by John Mitchell (1959)
   16-page text by E. Mitchell
   Distributor: Folkways Records (#8980)

This two-record set is a valuable guide to the meditation practice of Soto Zen as practiced at Eheiji temple which was founded by the great Zen master Dogen. The recordings follow the eighteen-hour-day of bells, drums, chanting, and recitation prescribed as part of the meditation practice of this tradition. The chants (mostly of many voices) include those for waking, donning robes, meals, recollections of vows, and voidness contemplation. The notes provide a detailed guide to the day's liturgy with descriptions of what is taking place, with whom, where, when, and why. Most of the chants have the Japanese originals given with an accompanying English translation. The text and recording, while not flawless, do reflect expert guidance, careful editing, and the full cooperation of the monastery. The recording is an unusual classroom listening experience and the notes provide a good introduction to Soto Zen meditation. Those who have the slide set *Zen* might use those visuals to supplement a classroom lecture.

CHAPTER 7

Buddhism in the West

Films

Art of Meditation
Awareness*
Buddhism, Man and Nature
Cathedral of the Pines: Buddhist Service 1976
Empowerment
Flow of Zen
Mood of Zen
New York Convention—1976
Pre-Bicentennial Convention in Blue Hawaii
Refuge
Zen and Now
Zen in America

* Reviewed in Section I: General and Historical Introductions

Films

Art of Meditation
   28 minutes, color, 16mm, 1971
   Sale $300.00, Rental $35.00
   Director/Producer: Irving and Elda Hartley
   Narrator: Alan Watts
   Distributor: Hartley Film Foundation
   Also available from: UIll, USoIll, Purdue, UWisc

In this film, Alan Watts presents his personal view of effective meditation. Based on his philosophy of life, the presentation portrays the essence of meditation as feeling or sensing "the present." While the film has Zen overtones, it does not describe any traditional Buddhist meditation practice: rather, Watts invites the viewer to participate in an eclectic array of meditation techniques, including breathing, chanting, identification with nature, and laughter. While viewing a series of picturesque scenes of streams, flowers, rocks, leaves, and birds, and while being called by voice, gong, and flute, the viewer is asked to experience the "reality of the Now" as the highest spiritual attainment. As such, this film can be considered to be an interpretation of such Buddhist concerns as the direct perception of reality, the necessity to shift one's consciousness for an insight into "the way things are," and the effort to replace doctrines and words by direct awareness. Any potential user should be alerted to the ending, which suggests that meditation (and perhaps life itself) should not be taken too seriously.

Many viewers will find this film enjoyable as a cinematographic experience and as a presentation of the plausibility and pleasure of meditation. It gives a glimpse of the late Alan Watts, one of the most notable popular exponents of Eastern philosophy in America during the second half of the twentieth century. Viewers should be cautioned about Watts' emphasis on immediate sensuous experience, and his reification of "the Now"—in contrast to the emphasis in Buddhism on pervasive moral and meditative disciplines and on the emptiness of all things, including "the Now." The film is suggestive of a syncretistic use of various Asian meditation techniques taken out of their historical and intellectual contexts. For a presentation of a more traditional Zen practice, see *Zen in Life.*

Buddhism, Man and Nature
   13 minutes, color, 16mm, 1968
   Sale $200.00, Rental $25.00
   Director/Producer: Irving and Elda Hartley

Narrator: Alan Watts
Series: Films for a New Age
Distributor: Hartley Film Foundation; also CC Films
Also available from: FlaSt, USoFla, UIll, UInd, UIowa, UMich, UMinn, PennSt, UWisc

In this film, Alan Watts interprets some Buddhist ideas in relation to his philosophy of life against the background of Chinese and Japanese painting, or scenes of flowing water, rocks, trees, and birds. He emphasizes that human life is one with nature, and that the process of life is just "what happens," so that a person need not be concerned for what ought to be. He advocates being awake to "the Now," watching the natural patterns of life unfold, and avoiding precise definitions of the order in nature.

The visual aspects of this film are effective. There is more explication of Watts' thought than in *Mood of Zen* or *Flow of Zen*. The direct relation of the film to Buddhism is found in the first few minutes when he discusses the Buddha's death, and refers to "Suchness" (tathata) as the most adequate expression of life. Viewers should be cautioned that in this film "Suchness" is interpreted as absorption into nature without explaining that for Zen Buddhism "nature" is empty. Similarly, Watts' advocacy of the need to stop thinking, and his emphasis on the recognition that life is not "going anywhere," oversimplifies the Buddhist concern to purify the mind, which is recognized traditionally as requiring great effort and extensive training as seen in *Zen in Life* and reel one of *Zen in Ryoko-in*. This film expresses a personal integration of key Buddhist and Taoist concepts with the American 1960s cultural movement of "letting go."

Cathedral of the Pines: Buddhist Service 1976
11 minutes, color, 16mm, 1976
Free rental
Producer: Wan-Go Weng
Distributor: Institute for the Advanced Studies of World Religions

This film depicts a Chinese-American Buddhist service at the Cathedral of the Pines in southern New Hampshire commemorating the American Bicentennial. It shows priests chanting in Chinese, bowing before Buddha images, praying for purification of the mind, and lay disciples presenting offerings. The service expresses praise to the Buddha, Dharma, and Sangha for the fact that Buddha's message has been brought to America. The footage includes brief excerpts of lectures by the head of the Buddhist Association of the United States, Rev. Sheng-Yen and C. T. Shen, the principle donor.

The photography is clear and colorful, and the soundtrack good. Some viewers might find the Chinese accent of the English narration difficult to understand. While the film lacks a general introduction to the underlying intention of a Buddhist ritual commemorating the bicentennial, it documents a Buddhist ritual used to celebrate an American event, and it provides a relatively detailed view of a communal Buddhist service.

Empowerment
   17 minutes, color, 16mm, 1976
   Sale inquire from distributor.
   Director/Producer: Mark Elliot and Victress Hitchcock
   Distributor: Vajradhatu Productions

This film documents the first visit in 1974 of the Karmapa Lama to the United States, including his arrival in Boulder, Colorado, and his visits to the West Coast and to the Hopi community in the Southwest. It is especially interesting as a record of American Buddhism, since much emphasis is placed on the preparations by American Buddhists for the visiting Lama. The "Black Crown Ceremony" is briefly shown, as is an Avalokiteshvara consecration ceremony.

Flow of Zen
   14 minutes, color, 16mm, 1969
   Sale $200.00, Rental $25.00
   Director: Irving and Elda Hartley
   Narrator: Alan Watts
   Series: Films for a New Age
   Distributor: Hartley Film Foundation
   Also available from: UIll, PennSt

This is a mood film in which Alan Watts interprets life's experiences in seemingly Taoist terms. He describes the world as "liquid movements," stressing that the never-ending change cannot be labeled or captured. In such a "dance in streaming liquid," religion is not something to hold onto, and God should not be conceived as solid rock or unchanging reality. The visual content includes abstract changing images of different colors—flowing, mixing, and turning in a fluid medium plus some natural scenes such as sea waves rushing over rocks, or shimmering reflections in water. During the last six or seven minutes, there is no narration, although throughout a background of sonorous music, a male chorus, and bells are integrated with the flowing imagery.

This is a pleasant sensual experience, excluding perhaps that last few minutes of unnarrated repeated views of changing abstract forms. The viewer must be aware that the title is misleading, since neither the cinematography nor the narration is concerned explicitly with the historical religious tradition of Zen. The overall impact suggests a Taoist perception of nature; for an Alan Watts film more suggestive of a Zen orientation, see *Buddhism, Man and Nature* or *Mood of Zen*.

Mood of Zen
   13 minutes, color, 16mm, 1967
   Sale $200.00, Rental $25.00
   Narrator: Alan Watts
   Producer: Elda Hartley
   Distributor: Hartley Film Foundation
   Also available from: UAriz, UInd, UIowa, PennSt, BYU, WashSt

In this film, Alan Watts presents Zen as living in a flow of energy. The film includes some beautiful scenes, including those of the Great Buddha of Kamakura, Nanzenji rock garden, and other Japanese gardens. It emphasizes the need for sensitivity to the spontaneous cooperation between humanity and nature, and the method of stilling the mind by which such sensitivity can be attained.

Overall, the film is visually and audially attractive, and it succeeds in creating a mood of serenity. This film confuses Zen teaching with a simple identity between humanity and nature, and Zen practice with an appreciation of nature and mere stillness. It omits basic traditional Zen interests in a dialectic of action and quietness, a disciplined ethical life, and regular meditative practice as is depicted in *Zen in Ryoko-in* and *Zen in Life*. This film is slightly more oriented toward intuition than Watts's *Buddhism, Man and Nature*, which has a bit more conceptual content. Both *Mood of Zen* and *Buddhism, Man and Nature* give a surer "feel" for Zen than so *Flow of Zen* and *Zen and Now*, the other films narrated by Alan Watts.

New York Convention—1976
   34 minutes, color, 16mm, 1976
   Sale none, Rental free
   Producer: NSA Productions
   Distributor: Nichiren Shoshu Academy

The visual content of this film is composed primarily of three forms of parade and pageantry celebrating the American Bicentennial on July third and fourth in New York City. The first shows excerpts of New York City's official Bicentennial Parade; the second is the presentation of a pageant, "The Spirit of '76," in Shea Stadium;

the third presents scenes of the Thirteenth General Meeting of the Nichiren Shoshu Academy (NSU) at the Louis Armstrong Memorial Stadium. Background music includes marching bands and sounds of celebration in the first segment, and an over-voice singing a hymn for commitment to the spirit of human spiritual revolution throughout the next 200 years—a central song in the pre-bicentennial pageant the year before. The final segment pertaining to the NSA General Meeting includes messages from the founder of NSA, Daisaku Ikeda, the general director of NSA, George M. Williams, and the then governor of Hawaii, the Honorable George R. Airyoshi.

This film documents the participation of NSA members in the American Bicentennial and the Thirteenth General Meeting of NSA in New York. Throughout, there are some general religious and ethical appeals for world peace and harmony given in background narrative; however, there are no distinctive Buddhist visual symbols or appeals to Nichiren thought and practice. The basic impression is of a Buddhist institution totally identified with American ideals.

Pre-Bicentennial Convention in Blue Hawaii
40 minutes, color, 16mm, 1975
Sale none, Rental free
Producer: NSA Productions
Distributor: Nichiren Shoshu Academy

Imaginative photography is combined with colorful extravaganzas of song and dance to portray the Twelfth General Meeting of the Nichiren Shoshu Academy in Honolulu, Hawaii. This is a film of conventioneers participating in disco and jazz entertainment, a parachutists' show, a night parade with floats depicting aspects of American life, and a water-and-stage ballet entitled "The Spirit of '76." It includes pictures of the founder of NSA, Daisaku Ikeda, and other dignitaries. The theme of the over-voice description is an affirmation of the American heritage, the goal of world peace, and the dignity of the individual.

The film documents the participation of one institutional form of Buddhism in contemporary American experience. There are no distinctive Buddhist symbols, temples, or rituals shown, and the narrative presents no identifiable Buddhist teachings.

This film is useful only as an example of NSA style—not of its Buddhist content or historical background.

Refuge
28 minutes, color, 16mm, 1973
Sale $325.00, Rental $35.00 & $7.00 shipping and handling charges

Director: Victress Hitchcock & Stephen Burchkardt
Producer: Tree Films
Distributor: Centre Productions, Inc.

This film depicts the members of the "Friends of the Western Buddhist Order" in England, under the direction of the Ven. Bikkhu Sangharakshita, meditating, living, and working together on the country estate that serves as their retreat. Interesting as a record of Buddhism in the West, the film includes many testimonials given by individuals as to why they have come to Buddhism, and how it has affected their lives.

Zen and Now
  14 minutes, color, 16mm, 1969
  Sale $200.00, Rental $25.00
  Director/Producer: Irving and Elda Hartley
  Narrator: Alan Watts
  Series: Films for a New Age
  Distributor: Hartley Film Foundation
  Also available from: UIll, PennSt, UWash

Color inundates the viewer as extraordinary photography captivates the senses. Frame upon frame of autumn leaves, flowers, floating objects on the smooth surface of a pond, various kinds of birds, berries, and vines make this an experience of "the unspeakable world." Through part of the film, Alan Watts encourages the viewer to avoid confusing the world of immediate sensory experience with ideas or concepts about it. He stresses that the viewer should let the senses engage one in a state of consciousness in which there is no past or future; there is only "Now."

This film is a photographic delight, but the viewer should be aware that Watts's emphasis on emptying the mind of words and thoughts ignores Zen's demand to empty the mind of attachment also to immediate sensuous enjoyment. Similarly, Watts fails to recognize the insight of the *Diamond Sutra*—which is studied in Zen temples—that there is not only no past nor future, there is no "Now" as such. For an Alan Watts's presentation which combines beautiful photography with a narration more directly related to Zen teaching, see his *Buddhism, Man and Nature*. For a film showing traditional Zen practice as it is related to contemporary Japaneses life, see *Zen in Life*.

Zen in America
  11minutes, color, 16mm, n.d.
  Sale inquire from distributor

Producer: Ralph Harper Silver for Amertat
Distributor: Cornerstone

This film is a separately produced and distributed presentation taken from a larger film entitled *Sunseed*—a film expressive of the "new age" religious consciousness of the late 1960s. Focusing on Zen as practiced at Tassajara Zen Center, an affiliate of the San Francisco Zen Center. *Zen in America* concentrates on interviews with the late Suzuki Roshi and some of his disciples, notably the current Roshi—Richard Baker. Interspersed with these interviews are scenes of meditation, chanting, eating, and working at the Zen Center. The Soto lineage of this particular Zen Center is evidenced in the characterization of Zen as a practice for "living totally in each moment," rather than seeking attainment.

The strength of this film lies more in its direct and rather appealing expression of "Zen personality" than in its descriptive or explanatory material. In fact, although Baker's comments are extensive, the film is worth seeing simply for its sequence on Shunryu Suzuki who radiates an authentic simplicity and joy, and suggests in the process that "too many words can ruin our life—we can't hear the birds sing!" Baker suggests that such radiance comes out of zazen, and out of the concentration in each moment.

This film is important as one of the few which points to a growing American Buddhism; however, it could also be used along with such films as *Zen in Life* or *Zen in Ryoko-in* as yet another expression of contemporary Zen practice. As such, it represents the presence on American soil of an authentic Zen practice and might be nicely contrasted with such films as Alan Watts' *Art of Meditation*.

I

Sources of Additional Materials

LISTED HERE are institutions and publications which might provide continuing guidance for locating other films, slides, and records not included in *Focus on Buddhism*.

The Asia Society, 725 Park Avenue, New York, NY 10021. The Education Program of The Asia Society produces occasional lists of films on Asia which may be of interest. The Society for Asian Music, affiliated with The Society, provides some discographic information, while The Performing Arts Council (described below) helps with the booking of Asian musical performances.

Audio-Visual Resource Guide, edited by Nick Abrams. New York; Friendship Press, 1972, 478 pp. $8.95. (Subtitled: "How to find the best in films, filmstrips, slides, records, tapes, picture sets, and other audiovisuals.") For schools, churches, and community organizations, this is one guide that does pay special attention to religion. One sub-section of the guide is devoted to religions of the Third World.

A Critical Guide to Curriculum Units and Audio-Visual Materials on China, prepared by the National Committee on U.S.-China Relations, 777 UN Plaza New York, NY 10017, 40 pp. This guide includes brief descriptions of about seventy-five films and reviews of slides, tapes, and other materials that were produced before 1970. It remains valuable as a better example of a critical survey than other later reviews, and because it is the most comprehensive survey of what was available by 1970. Many of the items described are not listed in later catalogues.

Educational Film Library Association, 43 West 61st Street, New York, NY 10023. The Association is a major clearinghouse of information on educational films, and sponsors the annual American Film Festival at which selected new educational films, including ethnographic films and films on religion, are screened and judged.

Educational Film Locator: The Consortium of University Film Centers, New York: R.R. Bowker Company, 1978, 2, 178 pp. This is a cross-listing of films available at fifty-two major university film libraries covering some 200,000 prints of over 37,000 titles. Each film is briefly described along with the date produced, the producer, the running time, and the audience level. In addition to including some of the films listed in this guide, the subject index of the *Educational Film Locator* should be consulted under India (200 films), China and Japan (200 films each), and other Asian countries (about 20 films on each). It should be noted that this valuable tool is a first attempt and contains errors and inconsistencies in such matters as: indexing some films on Christianity under "Religions, Eastern," and some Hinduism and Buddhist films under "Religions, Pagon." The addresses of publishers given at the back are seriously outdated. Despite these limitations, however, it is an invaluable guide to inexpensive rentals.

Film Resources on Japan, prepared by the University of Michigan Audio-Visual Education Center, Ann Arbor, MI. Washington: U.S. Govermnent Printing Office, 1975, 55 pp. Provides references to 355 films and 204 filmstrips on Japan. Some 250 films are given brief descriptive annotations, with a separate listing of films produced before 1960. There is a subject index listing 19 films on religion, most of which are reviewed in the present volume.

A Filmography of the Third World, compiled by Helen W. Cyr. Metuchen, NJ: Scarecrow Press, 1976, 319 pp. $12.50. This ambitious guide lists films distributed or available in the United States and Canada. Sources and complete cinematographic data are given along with one-sentence annotations. Some University film rental library collections are also listed. There are over 100 films on India, and more on Southeast Asia.

Films for Anthropology Teaching, compiled by Karl G. Heider. Washington, DC: American Anthropological Association, 1977, 3rd revised edition, 187 pp. $5.00. This guide provides an alphabetical annotated listing of about 780 films, indexed by geographic area (over 40 films on South Asia) and by topic, including sections on "ritual" and "lifecycle." Also included are descriptions of several films from the 1930s. Source data is given for all films.

Focus on Asian Studies, edited by Frank Buchanan. Published by the Service Center for Teachers of Asian Studies, Association for Asian Studies, The Ohio State University, 29 West Woodruff Avenue, Columbus, OH 43210 (Franklin R. Buchanan, Director). $2.00 per year. *Focus* is a quarterly guide to teaching materials in Asian studies, chiefly for high school use. It includes announcements and advertisements for new materials.

Guide to Slides on Asia, New York: The Asia Society, n.d., $1.30. A nine-page mimeographed listing of sources for buying slides, indicating general geographical areas in Asia handled by respective purveyors. No critical evaluations.

Japan Society, 333 East 47th St., New York, NY 10017. Through its film program, the Japan Society is the national leader in showing, promoting, and reviewing film resources on and from Japan. By arrangement with NHK-TV in Japan and Japanese producers, a number of films and videotapes are available from the Society for preview or purchase (contact Peter Grille, Director of Education). A comprehensive catalogue of film resources (approximately 400 films) is available.

The Journal of Ethnomusicology, Published by the Society for Ethnomusicology, 201 South Main Street, Room 513, Ann Arbor, MI 48108, *The Journal* reviews records and films of musical performances, and is a primary source for information concerning Asian religious music.

National Information Center for Educational Media (NICEM), University of Southern California, University Park, Los Angeles, CA 90007. NICEM catalogues provide the most comprehensive lists of educational films, video, and filmstrips. They are indexed under a variety of headings including "Philosophy" and "Religion." However, the user is always advised to check with the distributors of films directly to see if they are really available, since many films get into the catalogue without being successfully or long distributed.

New American Religions Project, Professor Frederick W. Blackwell and Jeff Zucker, New American Religions Project, Department of Foreign Languages, Washington State University, Pullman, WA 99164. This project is conducting a study of new age religious movements, focusing primarily upon groups centered around Eastern Religions, whether traditional or innovative. A guide with descriptive analyses of groups, bibliographies, and a comprehensive audio-visual listing is forthcoming. Currently, a listing of these Eastern-oriented groups and organizations is being maintained and copies are available for $2.00.

New York University Asian Studies Curriculum Center, Room 735, East Building, Washington Square, New York, NY 10003. The Asian Studies Curriculum Center has assembled a number of low-cost packages of teaching materials on Asia, including four slide sets on Buddhism reviewed in this volume. The materials were often prepared by curriculum specialists in conjunction with in-service training on Asia. Consequently, the pedagogical content is often very good and well suited to a variety of teaching situations.

Office of Tibet, 801 Second Avenue New York, NY 10017. The Office of Tibet was founded to represent the Dalai Lama in the 1960s appeal to the United Nations on behalf of Tibet. The Office has since changed its function to provide information and act as a liaison for interested groups, organizations, and individuals. It has some films for rent and is a good source of up-to-date information on audio-visual materials on Tibet.

Oriental Music: A Selected Discography, Jacques Brunet, ed. (compiled by International Institute for Comparative Music Studies in Berlin). Available through Learning Resources in International

Studies, Suite 1231, 60 East 42nd Street, New York, NY 10017, 1971, 100 pp. $3.00 (FAMC Occasional Publication No. 16). This catalogue of some 300 recordings devoted to traditional Asian music is aimed at providing basic information on available materials—mostly those issued in Asian countries. Includes titles, sources, historical background, and descriptions of instruments used by performers, with notes by ten regional specialists.

The Performing Arts Council, The Asia Society, 725 Park Avenue, New York, NY 10021. The Performing Arts Council sponsors. U.S. tours by Asian dance companies and maintains loan collections of films and videocassettes of these performances.

Slide Buyers Guide, edited by Nancy Delaurier, 3rd revised edition, New York: The College Art Association, 1976. The College Art Association of America, 16 East 52nd Street, New York, NY 10022. This work lists the major suppliers of art slides, and gives general information on their prices, catalogues, business practices, and the quality of their slides. There is a subject index referring the reader to the suppliers of slides. For example, under geographical areas, twenty-nine dealers are listed for slides on India (seven are overseas). The introduction gives helpful information on evaluating, buying and preserving slides, and on color fidelity and retention of various reproduction techniques.

Tibetan Resources in North America, Published by the Himalayas Council of The Asia Society, 125 Park Avenue, New York, NY 10021, 1979, 42 pp. $4.00. (Occasional Paper #3.) This is a comprehensive descriptive listing of institutions and key individuals involved in education about Tibetan culture.

University and College Film Collections: A Directory, compiled by Indiana University Audio Visual Center and Consortium of University Film Centers, New York. Educational Film Library Association, 43 West 61st Street, New York, NY 10023, 1974, 76 pp. $7.00. This is a state-by-state listing of 415 film collections, giving the size of the collection, addresses, and availability for rental. Collections listed range in size from under 100 films to over 10,000. The *Educational Film Locator,* listed above, indexes the holdings of fifty of the larger libraries.

Additional Sources of Films, Slides, and Recordings

Above and beyond the audio-visual materials reviewed in this guide, there are many more that might conceivably be used for teaching about the different Asian cultures involved with Buddhism. Listed here are sources of significant quantities of films, slides, and records which do not directly pertain to Buddhism, but may be of interest to some. Readers should also consult the listing of *Sources for Additional Information.*

Films

Encyclopedia Ethnographica, American Archive, The Pennsylvania State University, Audio Visual Services, 17 Willard Building, University Park, PA 16802. This is a film-lending archive, primarily of silent films of ethnographic importance. Films generally come with a guide or monograph, and many are under five minutes in length. Film rental prices seem to average about $1.00 per minute.

Film Australia, Australian Consulate-General, 636 Fifth Avenue, New York, NY 10020. In addition to the films reviewed in this volume, Film Australia has produced a number of films on Asian countries in its "Our Neighbor Series" which includes brief films on particular topics in India, Southeast Asia, and Indonesia (see reviews of *Chiang Mai, Northern Capital* and *Temple of the Twenty Pagodas*). Its "Asian Insight Series" includes *Thailand* (reviewed in this guide) and five other 52-minute films on Asian countries.

Hong Kong Tourist Association, 548 Fifth Avenue, New York, NY 10036. Approximately twenty films are available on life in Hong Kong. These films are loaned free of charge, but should be ordered one month in advance.

India: Government of, (Northeast and Midwest) Consulate General of India, 3 East 64th Street, New York, NY 10021; (South) Information Services of India, 2107 Massachusetts Avenue, N.W., Washington, DC 20008; (West) Consulate General of India, 215 Market Street, San Francisco, CA 94105. The Government of India has a large number of films which may be obtained for showing free. However, distribution is unreliable, the physical quality of the prints is often poor, and the information dealing with social issues may be misleading. Inquiries regarding the purchase of prints of films produced by or for the Films Division, Government of India, should be addressed to the following agency: National Education and Information Films Ltd., National House Tulloch Road, Appolo Bunde, Bombay-26, India.

Japan Society, See Sources for Additional Information (above).

Korean Consulate General, Office of Cultural Information, 460 Park Avenue, New York, NY 10021. They have a large number of films available on a variety of subjects concerning modern Korea, tourism, and Korean art.

Office of Tibet, 801 Second Avenue, New York, NY 10017. In addition to the films reviewed in this volume (e.g., *The Lama King*), the Office of Tibet also has other films available for rent on the Tibetan community in exile and anticipates getting more in the future.

The Performing Arts Council, The Asia Society. 725 Park Avenue, New York, NY 10021. The Council has currently over a dozen films and videotapes available for loan or sale on Asian dance, mostly Indian. Those seen were filmed on a bare stage with limited technical facilities, performed by visiting artists on tour in the United States under Asia

Society sponsorship. This collection is expected to grow. (Note that the Council may be able to assist in booking actual performances.)

Tourism Authority of Thailand, 5 World Trade Center, New York, NY 10048. Currently, this organization loans five films on Thailand without charge. Requests for films should be made at least three weeks in advance.

Tribune Films, 38 West 32nd Street, New York, NY 10001. Tribune Films handles films for the Government of Sri Lanka. These are available on loan without charge, but advance booking is recommended.

University Film Rental Libraries, These are the *first* sources a teacher should look to for low-cost film rentals. University film libraries seldom have more than one print of a film, however, and the potential user should make sure the film will be available on the day which he wants it; this also makes it difficult to be sure of having time to preview a film before showing it. The Syracuse University film catalogue states that priority is assigned to orders as received and that requests for the following year start arriving at Syracuse in March. (Note that currently 415 libraries are listed in *University and College Film Collections: A Directory*, and holdings of 450 libraries are listed in the *Educational Film Locator* [see section on Sources for Additional Information]).

Slides

(See also *Guide to Slides on Asia* and *Slide Buyers Guide* in Sources for Additional Information section)

American Committee for South Asian Art (ACSAA). There is a continuing series of slides being issued in sets of 100 each year by ACSAA. Since they are prepared by and for art historians, the slides are of generally excellent visual quality, if not directly related to the study of religion. However, since much South Asian Art is religious (including Buddhist), these sets may be very useful for the instructor who can prepare suitable background notes for the slides. The minimal identifications that come with ACSAA slides are a barrier to their use by nonspecialists. See reviews of *Early Buddhist Art of the Stupas, Himalayan Art,* and *Ajanta . . . . ,* and appendix on distributors for ACSAA addresses.

Dr. Block Color Reproduction, 1309 North Genesee Avenue, Hollywood, CA 90046. Lists sets on Art of India (60 slides, including Nepal), Southeast Asia, 257 slides) and Japanese art (107 slides). Cost is about $1.25 per slide.

Honolulu Academy of Arts, Academy Shop, 900 South Beretonia Street, Honolulu, HI 96814. Lists approximately 75 slides of Asian art at 75¢ each.

Interbook Inc. 13 East 16th Street, New York, NY 10003. Distributes a few slide sets on Asia produced by The Asia Society, Sackler Foundation (on Chinese bronzes), and the Foreign Area Materials Center (on South Asia).

Kai Dib Films International, P.O. Box 261, Glendale, CA 91209. In addition to *Philosophy of Zen* (reviewed in this guide), Kai Dib has a number of lecture/slide sets available of interest on Asian culture. Among these sets are "East-West" (260 slides juxtaposing more or less comparable views of art and ordination from Occident and Oreint); "Korea" (260 slides with lecture notes on Korean art history), "Oriental Theatre" (85 slides, 10-page guide), and "Archaeological Finds of the People's Republic of China" (190 slides with only a few pieces on Buddhism). Slides are $1.95 each with complete sets at 25% discount. Sets may be previewed on a thirty-day approval basis.

Los Angeles County Museum of Art, Museum Shop, 5905 Wilshire Boulevard Los Angeles, CA 90036. The Los Angeles Museum lists four slide sets of five slides each on Indian (#12), Indo-Tibetan (#13), and Oriental (#18 and 19). Each set is $1.50.

Museum of Art, University of Oregon, Eugene, OR 97403. Approximately 100 slides of oriental art at 75¢ each.

Neil Hart, 500 Northeast 12th Avenue, Hallandale, FL 33009. He has a large assortment of slides on Asian art, religious sites, festivals, and landscapes. His current listing includes more than 100 slides on Ladakh, 200 on Nepal, 200 on Thailand, 100 on Sri Lanka, and a few on Buddhist sites in Japan, India, and Afghanistan. Hart promises quality reproductions at $2.50 per slide.

Prothman Associates, Inc., 650 Thomas Avenue, Baldwin, NY 11510. Prothman produces slides and imports sets from twenty-five foreign companies. The slides vary greatly in quality according to the producer and their age, but include a number of worthwhile sets and individual slides on Asian art in addition to *L'Art Khmer, The Arts of Japan, History of the Oriental Arts*, and *Nara and Kyoto*, all reviewed in the present volume. Prices are $1.95 for individual slides and less for sets.

Recordings

Folkways Records: Mail Order Catalogue, Write to Folkways Records, 43 West 61st Street, New York, NY 10023. This ten-page catalogue of nearly 2,000 titles includes well over 100 recordings of Asian music, including art music of Japan, China, Korea, and Southeast Asia. Folkways' printed guides supplied with some records are generally much more helpful than the notes found on most record jackets. Many recordings go back to the early 1950s and have been continually available.

The Full Circle Archive, P.O. Box 4370, Boulder, CO 80306 provides a cooperative distribution and lending service to members, to whom tapes and videocassettes may be rented for $1 plus postage. Currently, their catalogue ($2, which can be applied to the $12 membership fee) lists about 500 items, ranging from "A Conversation with Joseph Campbell" to "Zen: The Eternal"

Lyrichord Records, 140 Perry Street, New York, NY 10014. Lyrichord is becoming a leading producer of recorded Asian music with substantial listings of Japanese, Chinese, Southeast Asian, and Himalayan music in addition to the items reviewed in this book. Lyrichord intends to expand its offerings in the near future. A complete catalogue of ethnographic music (mostly Asian) is available upon request.

Nonesuch Records, 665 Fifth Avenue, New York, NY 10022. Especially in its Explorer series, Nonesuch Records represents a rich resource for recordings of authentic Asian religious art and music. Check your local record shops before writing; Nonesuch has a good distribution network.

Pacifica Audio Programs & Pacifica Tape Library, 5316 Venice Blvd., Los Angeles, CA 90019. Selected interview and other public information format programs from the Pacifica radio network stations are available for purchase. Of over 15,000 programs in the archive, approximately one-sixth have been announced in annotated catalogues. The two most recent are available for $1 each and list over 1,000 programs, including a number on India, modern religious movements, and world religions. Both the library and the catalogues are expanding and this is likely to be an increasing significant source of radio (especially educational radio) programs. Tapes are for sale on either reel or cassette, and average $12 for a one-hour program.

Unipub, 345 Park Avenue South, New York, NY 10010 This is the offical U.S. distributor for many UN and UN-sponsored materials, including the UNESCO series of books and records, as well as a number of slide sets on the art of the non-Western world. Some of these materials have been reviewed elsewhere in this volume.

Distributors of Films, Slide Sets, and Recordings Used in This Guide

Academic Support Center Film Library
The University of Missouri—Columbia
505 East Stewart Road
Columbia, MO 65211

ACI, c/o Paramount Communications
5451 Marathon Street
Hollywood, CA 90038

American Committee for South Asian Art
c/o I. Job Thomas
Asian Studies Department
Davidson College
Davidson, NC 28026
or:
ACSAA Slide Project
Department of Art History
Tappan Hall
University of Michigan
Ann Arbor, MI 48109

Argus Communications
7440 Natchez Avenue
Niles, IL 60648

The Asia Society
725 Park Avenue
New York, NY 10021

Asian Studies Curriculum Center
New York University
Room 735, East Building
Washington Square
New York, NY 10003

Australian Information Services
Australian Consulate General
636 Fifth Avenue
New York, NY 10020

Bailey Films Associates
(BFA Educational Media)
2211 Michigan Avenue
P.O. Box 1795
Santa Monica, CA 90406

Benchmark Films
145 Scarborough Road
Briarcliff Manor, NY 10510

CC Films
National Council of Churches
Room 860
475 Riverside Drive
New York, NY 10027

Budek Films and Slides
1023 Waterman Avenue
East Providence, RI 02914

Carousel Films, Inc.
1501 Broadway
New York, NY 10036

Centre Productions
1312 Pine Street
Boulder, CO 80302

Centron Educational Films
1621 Ninth Street—Box 687
Lawrence, KS 66044

Consulate General of India/Information Services of India (*See* India, Government of)

Contemporary/McGraw-Hill Films
1221 Avenue of the Americas
New York, NY 10020

Cornerstone Films
Sale: Attention: Fred Cohen
811 18th Street
Boulder, CO 80307
Rental: 470 Park Avenue South
New York, NY 10016

East Coronet
65 East Southwater St.
Chicago, IL 60601

Department of South Asian Studies
Distribution Office
1242 Van Hise Hall
1220 Linden Avenue
University of Wisconsin—Madison
Madison, WI 53706

Far Eastern Audio Visual
P.O. Box 543
Cedar Park, TX 78613

Film Images/Radim Films
1034 Lake Street
Oak Park, IL 60301

Films Incorporated
733 Greenbay Road
Wilmette, IL 60091

Focus International, Inc.
1776 Boradway
New York, NY 10019

Folkways Records
43 West 61st Street
New York, NY 10023

Government of India
(*see* India, Government of)

Hartley Film Foundation
Cat Rock Road
Cos Cob, CT 06807

India, Government of (for free viewing, *see also* Public Service Audience Planners, Inc. which may have some Government of India films)
Purchase: National Education and Information Films Ltd. National House
Tulloch Road
Appolo Bunder
Bombay-26, India

Rental:
Northeast & Midwest U.S.
Consulate General of India
3 East 64th Street
New York, NY 10021
Southern U.S.
Information Services of India
2107 Massachusetts Avenue, NW
Washington, DC 20008
Western U.S.
Consulate General of India
215 Market Street
San Francisco, CA 94105

Indiana University
Audio Visual Center
Bloomington, IN 47401

Information Services of India
(*See* India, Government of)

Institute for the Advanced Studies of World Religions
2150 Center Avenue
Fort Lee, NJ 07024

Interbook, Inc.
13 East 16th Street
New York, NY 10003

International Film Bureau, Inc.
332 South Michigan Avenue
Chicago, IL 60604

International Film Foundation, Inc.
475 Fifth Avenue
Suite 916
New York, NY 10017

Iwanami Productions
22-2 Kanda Misakicho
Chiyada-ku
Tokyo, Japan

Japan Foundation
Suite 570
Watergate Office Building
600 New Hampshire Avenue, NW
Washington, DC 20037

Japan Society, Inc.
333 East 47th Street
New York, NY 10017

Kai Dib Films International
P.O. Box 261
Glendale, CA 91209

Korean Consulate
Cultural Information Service
460 Park Avenue
New York, NY 10022

Lyrichord Records
141 Perry Street
New York, NY 10014

Macmillan Films, Inc.
34 MacQuesten Parkway South
Mt. Vernon, NY 10550

Mass Media Ministries
2116 North Charles St.
Baltimore, MD 21218

McGraw-Hill Films
1221 Avenue of the Americas
New York, NY 10020

National Council of Churches
(see CC Films)

National Film Board of Canada
1251 Avenue of the Americas
New York, NY 10020

Navin Kumar, Inc.
967 Madison Avenue
New York, NY 10021

New York University
Asian Studies Curriculum Center
Room 735, East Building
Washington Square
New York, NY 10003

Nichiren Shoshu Academy (NSA)
5525 Wilshire Blvd.
Santa Monica, CA 90401

Nonesuch Records
665 Fifth avenue
New York, NY 10022

Office of Tibet
801 2nd Avenue
New York, NY 10017

The Ohio State University
(See Service Center for Teachers of
   Asian Studies)

Orient Films Association
Kyodo Nihon Bashi Building
2 - Moro Machi
1 - Chome
Nihon Bashi
Tokyo, Japan

The Pennsylvania State University
Audio Visual Services
Special Services Bldg.
University Park, PA 16802

Permanent Mission of Bhutan
866 2nd Avenue
New York, NY 10017

Peter M. Robeck and Co.
Dist. by Time Life Video Inc.
100 Eisenhower Drive
Paramus, NJ 07652

Pictura Film Distribution Corp.
118 8th Avenue
New York, NY 10011

Prothman Associates
650 Thomas Avenue
Baldwin, NY 11510

Public Service Audience
   Planners, Inc.
   East:
      1 Rockefeller Plaza
      New York, NY 10020
   Midwest:
      645 North Michigan Avenue
      Chicago, IL 60611
   West:
      6290 Sunset Boulevard
      Hollywood, CA 90028

Radim Films/Film Images
(see Film Images/Radim Films)

Ruth Stephan Films
c/o Macmillan Films, Inc.
34 MacQuesten Parkway South
Mt. Vernon, NY 10550

Sakura Motion Picture Co.

Scholarly Publications
   (formerly Sheikh Productions)
5 Beekman Street
New York, NY 10038

Service Center for Teachers
   of Asian Studies
The Ohio State University
29 Woodruff Avenue
Columbus, OH 43210

Social Studies Schools Service
10000 Culver Boulevard
Culver City, CA 90230

Sterling Educational Films
241 East 34th Street
New York, NY 10016

Thread Cross Films
Pulteney Mews
Bath, Avon BA2 4DS
England

Threshold Films
2025 North Highland Avenue
Hollywood, CA 90068

Time Life Video, Inc.
100 Eisenhower Drive
Paramus, NJ 07652

Tribune Films
38 West 32nd Street
New York, NY 10001

UNIPUB
345 Park Avenue South
New York, NY 10010

University of California—Berkeley
Extension Media Center
2223 Fulton Street
Berkeley, CA 94720

University of Illinois
Audio Visual Services
1325 South Oak Street
Champaign, IL 61820

University of Michigan
Audio-Visual Education Center
416 4th Street
Ann Arbor, MI 48103

University of Mid-America
Marketing Division
1600 North 33rd Street
P.O. Box 82006
Lincoln, NE 68501

University of Missouri—Columbia
(*see* Academic Support Center
Film Library)

University of Washington
Instructional Media Services
University of Washington
Seattle, WA 98195

University of Wisconsin
(*see* Department of South Asian
Studies

Vajradhatu Productions
1345 Spruce Street
Boulder, CO 80302

Visual Education Service
Yale University Divinity School
409 Prospect Street
New Haven, CT 06511

Yale University School
(*see* Visual Education Service)

Xerox Films
245 Long Hill Road
Middletown, CT 06457

Lending Libraries

Key to "Also available from" institutional sources mentioned and listed alphabetically *by order of state* within text.

Arizona:
　ArizSt
　　Arizona State
　　Central Arizona Film
　　Cooperative
　　Audiovisual Center
　　Tempe, AZ 85281
　　602/965-5073

UAriz
　University of Arizona
　Bureau of Audio-
　　Visual Services
　Tucson, AZ 85706
　602/884-3282

California
UCB
University of
California/Berkeley
Extension Media Center
2223 Fulton Street
Berkeley, CA 94720
415/642-0460
UCLA
University of
California/Los Angeles
Instructional Media
Library
Royce Hill 8
405 Hilgard Avenue
Los Angeles, CA 90024
213/825-0755

Colorado:
UCol
University of Colorado
Educational Media Center
348 Stadium Bldg.
Boulder, CO 80302
303/492-7341

Connecticut:
UCt
University of Connecticut
Center for Instructional
Media & Technology
Storrs, CT 06268
203/486-2530

Florida
FlaSt
Florida State University
Instructional Support Center
Film Library
030 Seminole Dining Hall
Tallahassee, FL 32306
904/644-2820
USoFla
University of South Florida
Film Library
4202 Fowler Avenue
Tampa, FL 33620
813/974-2874
(Kate Reynolds, Director)

Idaho:
Boise
Boise State University
Educational Media Services
1910 Colorado Blvd.
Boise, ID 83706
208/385-3289
Idaho St
Idaho State University
Audio Visual Services
Campus Box 80604
Pocatello, ID 83209
208/236-3212

Illinois:
NoIll
Northern Illinois University
Media Distribution Department
De Kalb, IL 60115
815/753-0171
SoIll
Southern Illinois University
Learning Resources Services
Carbondale, IL 62901
618/453-2258
UIll
University of Illinois
Visual Aids Service
1325 South Oak Street
Champaign, IL 61820
217/333-1360

Indiana:
IndSt
Indiana State University
Audio Visual Center
Stalker Hill
Terre Haute, IN 47807
812/232-6311
IndU
Indiana University
Audio Visual Center
Bloomington, IN 47401
812/337-2103
Purdue
Purdue University
Audio Visual Center
Stewart Center
West Lafayette, IN 47907
317/749-6188

Iowa:
IowaSt
Iowa State University
Media Resource Center
121 Pearson Hall
Ames, IA 50010
515/249-8022
UIowa
University of Iowa
Audio Visual Center
C-5 East Hall
Iowa City, IA 52242
319/353-5885

Kansas:
UKans
South Asia Program
University of Kansas
Manhattan, KS 66502

Maine:
UMe
University of Maine
Instructional Systems Center
16 Shibles Hall
Orono, ME 04473
207/581-7541

Massachusetts:
BU
Boston University
Krasker Memorial
Film Library
765 Commonwealth Avenue
Boston, MA 02215
617/353-3272

Michigan:
UMich
University of Michigan
Audio Visual Education Center
416 Fourth Street
Ann Arbor, MI 48103
313/764-5360

Minnesota:
UMinn
University of Minnesota
Audio Visual Library Services
3300 University Avenue, SE
Minneapolis, MN 55414
612/373-3810

Missouri:
UMo
University of Missouri
Academic Support Center
505 East Stewart Road
Columbia, MO 65211
314/882-3601

Nebraska:
UNeb
University of Nebraska/
Lincoln
Instructional Media Center
Nebraska Hall 421
Lincoln, NE 68588
402/472-1911

Nevada:
University of Nevada

New York:
NYU
New York University Audio-
Visual Center
Washington Square
New York, NY 10003
SyrU
Syracuse University
Film Rental Center
1455 East Colvin Street
Syracuse, NY 13210
315/479-6631

North Carolina:
NoCarSt
North Carolina State University
at Raleigh
Raleigh, NC 27607
UNoCar
University of North Carolina
Bureau of Audio Visual
Education
P.O. Box 2228
Chapel Hill, NC 27514
919/933-1108

Ohio:
KentSt
Kent State University
Audio Visual Services
330 Library Bldg.
Kent, OH 44242
216/672-3456

Oklahoma:
OklaSt
Oklahoma State University
A-V Center
Stillwater, OK 74074
405/624-7212

Pennsylvania:
PennSt
The Pennsylvania State
University
Audio Visual Services
Special Services Bldg.
University Park, PA 16802
814/865-6314

South Carolina:
USoCar
University of South Carolina
Audio Visual Services
Columbia, SC 29208
803/777-2858

Tennessee:
UTenn
University of Tennessee
Teaching Materials Center
R-61 Communications
Knoxville, TN 37916
615/974-3236

Texas:
UTex
University of Texas at Austin
General Libraries Film Library
Box W
Austin, TX 78712
512/471-3573

Utah:
BYU
Brigham Young University
Educational Media Center
290 Herald R. Clark Bldg.
Provo, UT 84602
801/374-1211 (x3456)

Washington:
WashSt
Washington State University
Instructional Media Services
Pullman, WA 99164
509/335-4535
UWash
University of Washington/
Seattle
Instructional Media Services
23 Kane Hall DG-10
Seattle, WA 98195
206/543-9909

Wisconsin:
UWisc
University of Wisconsin/
Madison
Bureau of Audio-Visual
Instruction
1327 University Avenue
Madison, WI 53706
608/262-1644

Wyoming:
UWy
University of Wyoming
Audio Visual Services
Box 3273 University Station
Room 14, Knight Hall
Laramie, WY 82071

Selected Index of Film Makers, Narrators, Series (Films and Videocassettes)

ACI (c/o Paramount
  Communications)
  Kyudo: Japanese Ceremonial
    Archery
JOHN ADAIR
  The Path
PIERRE ALECHINSKY
  Japanese Calligraphy
ALLIED ARTISTS LONDON &
& SNOWLION COMMUNICA-
TIONS
  Tantra of Gyuto
ALTARS OF THE WORLD
  Buddhism and Shintoism in Japan
  Mahayana Buddhism
  Theravada Buddhism
ARTS OF THE ORIENT
  Thai Images of the Buddha
ASIAN INSIGHT
  Thailand
LEW AYERS
  Buddhism and Shintoism in Japan
  Mahayana Buddhism
  Theravada Buddhism
BACH-HORIZON
  Japan: Land of the Kami
JACKSON BAILEY
  Japan: The Living Tradition—
    "Religious Experience" (Part I)
  Japan: The Living Tradition—
    "Religious Experience" (Part II)
JAMES BEVERIDGE
  Buddhism

STEPHAN BEYER
  Himalayan Buddhism
M. BHAVNANI
  Cave Temples of India—Buddhist
  Land of Enlightenment
ROGER BLAIR
  Angkor: The Lost City
BRIAN BLAKE
  Borobudur: The Cosmic Mountain
SERGE BOURGUIGNON
  The Smile
BROADCASTING
PROGRAMMING CENTER
OF JAPAN
  Buddhist Art
JULIEN BRYAN
  The Ancient Chinese
STEPHEN BURCHKARDT
  Refuge
ARUN CHAUDHURI
  Nalanda
CHINA FILM ENTERPRISES
OF AMERICA
  Chinese Sculpture
    through the Ages
CHINA INSTITUTE IN AMERICA
  Buddhism in China
CHINESE CULT OF THE DEAD
(PART II)
  Journey into the Night:
    Chinese Funeral Rites

IWANAMI PRODUCTIONS
Horyuji Temple
Zen Training of a Young Monk

VIRENDRA KUMAR JAIN
Lama Dances of Tibet

JOHN JAMES
The Buddha in South Asia

JAPAN: THE LIVING TRADITION
Japan: The Living Tradition—
"Religious Experience" (Part I)
Japan: The Living Tradition—
"Religious Experience" (Part II)

M. K. JOHNS
Tibetan Story

LARRY JORDAN
Sacred Art of Tibet

VANYA KEWLEY
The Lama King

K. L. KHANDPUR
Ladakh
Malanda

RAJBANS KHANNA
Gautama the Buddha

KIROKU EIGASHA
PRODUCTIONS
Nara and Kyoto: The Cultural
Heritage of Japan

ELSEBET KJOLBYE
Vejen

DAVID KNIPE
The Buddha in South Asia
Himalayan Buddhism

TOKUZO KNODO
The Spider's Thread

KOREAN FILM BOARD
Pulguksa Temple

KOREAN FILM PRODUCTIONS
Religions of Korea

DAVID LASCELLES
A Prophecy

FRANZ LASI FILM (STUTTGART)
Bhutan—Land of the
Peaceful Dragon

XENIA LISANEVICH
Sherpa High Country

THE LONG SEARCH
Buddhism: Land of the
Disappearing Buddha—Japan
Buddhism: Footprint of the
Buddha—India

MIKKI MAHER
Tibetan Medicine: A Buddhist
Approach to Healing

ADRIAN MALONE
The Glory That Remains

MATSUDAI
Hiraizumi: Capital of the North

MATSUOKA PRODUCTIONS
Ryokan: The Poet Priest

EZRA MIR
Nagarjunakonda

PETER MONTAGNON
Buddhism: Footprint of the
Buddha—India
Buddhism: Land of the
Disappearing Buddha—Japan

EDWARD P. MORGAN
The Gods of Japan

JOHN MORRIS
Chiang Mai, Northern Capital
Temple of the Twenty Pagodas

JAGAT MURARI
Cave Temples of India—Buddhist

EDWARD R. MURROW
Burma, Buddhism and Neutralism

NEPAL: LAND OF THE GODS
Sherpa Legend
The Tantric Universe
Tibetan Heritage

PAUL NEVIN
Burma, Buddhism and Neutralism

NHK JAPAN
BROADCASTING COMPANY
Hiraizumi: Capital of the North
Jizo Children's Festival
Restoration of the Golden Shrine
Smiling Images of the Buddha
The Spider's Thread
Spirit of Zen
Torches of Todaiji
Woodblock Mandala:
The World of Shiko Munakata
Yakushiji Temple:
The Cream of the Buddhist Arts

ARCH NICHOLSON
  Thailand
NIHON FILM CENTER
  Zen in Life
NSA PRODUCTIONS
  New York Convention—1976
  Pre-Bicentennial Convention
    in Blue Hawaii
OFFICE OF TIBET
  The Religious Investiture of
    H. H. the Dalai Lama
OMOTO FOUNDATION
  Art and Spirit
OUR ASIAN NEIGHBORS
  Chiang Mai, Northern Capital
  Temple of the Twenty Pagodas
ROBERT M. PERRY
  The Buddhist World
E. O. REISCHAUER
  Japan: The Living Tradition—
    "Religious Experience" (Part I)
  Japan: The Living Tradition—
    "Religious Experience" (PartII)
THE RELIGIONS OF MAN
  Buddhism
SHELDON ROCHLIN
  Sherpa Legend
  Tantra of Gyuto
  The Tantric Universe
  Tibetan Heritage
  Tibetan Medicine: A Buddhist
    Approach to Healing
YSBRAND ROGGE
  Zen Facets of Japanese Religion
BIMAL ROY
  Gautama the Buddha
  Immortal Stupa
SAKURA MOTION
PICTURE COMPANY
  Noh Drama
S. N. S. SASTRY
  Nagarjunakonda
ALEXANDER SCOURBY
  Buddhism in China
JOHN SEABOURNE
  Thailand: Land of Smiles
GARY SEAMAN
  Journey into the Night:
    Chinese Funeral Rites

SERMONS IN STONE
  The Glory That Remains
KEITH SHACKLETON
  Bhutan—Land of the
    Peaceful Dragon
SHIN NIPPON PRODUCTIONS
  Nara, Japan
KANATSU SHUNJI
  Gen: Mystery of Mysteries
RALPH HARPER SILVER
  Zen in America
SINCINKIN
  Haiku
HUSTON SMITH
  Buddhism
  Requiem for a Faith
SNOWLION
COMMUNICATIONS
  (see Allied Artists London)
THANOM SOONARATNA
  Chiang Mai, Northern Capital
  Temple of the Twenty Pagodas
GIL SORENSON
  Awareness
RUTH STEPHAN
  Zen in Ryoko-in
PHILIP STRAPP
  The Ancient Chinese
SUMAI FILMS
  The Path
JIGME TARING
  The Religious Investiture
    of H. H. the Dalai Lama
JOHN TEMPLE
  Thailand
LOWELL THOMAS (SR./JR.)
  Our of This World:
    Forbidden Tibet
  Pearl of the East
LOWELL THOMAS, JR.
  Out of This World:
    Forbidden Tibet
TREE FILMS
  Refuge
A TRILOGY ON TIBET:
TIME BEFORE, TIME BEING,
TIME AFTER (PART I)
  A Prophecy

UNIVERSITY OF MID-AMERICA
Japan: The Living Tradition—
"Religious Experience" (Part I)
Japan: The Living Tradition—
"Religious Experience" (Part II)
UNIVERSITY OF WASHINGTON
ARCHIVES OF ETHNIC
MUSIC AND DANCE
Buddhist Dances of Korea
U.S. OFFICE OF EDUCATION
Arts of Japan: Bridge of Beauty
SHANTI VARMA
A King Is Crowned
Ladakh
ZUL VELLANI
Nalanda
MOHAN WADHWANI
Land of Enlightenment
ALAN WATTS
Art of Meditation
Buddhism, Man and Nature
Flow of Zen
Mood of Zen
Zen and Now

ANDREW WELSH
Haiku

WAN-GO WENG
Buddhism in China
Cathedral of the Pines:
Buddhist Service 1976
China: The Golden Age
China: The Great Cultural Mix
China: The Heavenly Khan
Chinese Sculpture through
the Ages

WORLD CULTURAL
GEOGRAPHY
ASIAN NOTEBOOK
Thailand: Land of Smiles

WORLD OF LOWELL THOMAS
Pearl of the East

BASIL WRIGHT
Song of Ceylon

PAUL ZILS
Meditation

Index of Topics and Terms

Films listed in the Index are not necessarily recommended; such listing indicates only that a film treats a particular name, term, or topic. The review may indicate that this treatment, or the entire film, is inadequate.

Films	**Slides and Recordings** [Recordings are denoted by (R)]
AESTHETICS	
Japanese	
Art and Spirit	*Philosophy of Zen*
Arts of Japan . . .	
Gen . . .	
The Path	
Spirit of Zen	
Zen in Ryoko-in	
Tibetan	
Meditation Crystallized	*The Art of Tibet* *Sacred Art of Tibet*
Tibet	
ALMS-GIVING/ALMS-ROUNDS *(see also* MONK/LAITY INTERACTION)*	
Buddhism: Be Ye Lamps . . .	
Buddhism: Footprint of the *Buddha—India*	*Monk's Ordination Ceremony*
I Am a Monk	
Temple of the Twenty Pagodas	
Theravada Buddhism	
Tibetan Heritage	
Vejen	
AMERICAN BUDDHISM	
Art of Meditation	
Cathedral of the Pines . . .	
Empowerment	
New York Convention—1976	
Pre-Bicentennial . . .	
Refuge	
Zen in America	
ANGKOR	
Angkor Wat: The Lost City	*L'Art Khmer*
Angkor Wat: The Ancient City	
ARCHEOLOGY	
Borobudur . . .	*Early Buddhist Art . . .*
Buddhism in China	
Nagarjunakonda	

Chinese
  Buddhism in China   *Buddhism*
  Buddhist Art   *Chinese Religions*
  China: The Golden Age   *History of the Oriental Arts*
Folk Arts
  Chinese Legends . . .
  Smiling Images of the Buddha
  Vesak
Himalayan
  Sacred Art of Tibet   *The Art of Tibet*
                       Himalayan Art
                       Tibetan Art Set
                       Tibetan Buddhism

Indian
  Cave Temples of   *Ajanta . . .*
    India—Buddhist
  The Glory That Remains   *Buddhism*
  Immortal Stupa   *Early Buddhist Art . . .*
  Land of Enlightenment   *Evolution of the Buddha Image*
  Nagarjunakonda   *The Great Stupa at Sanchi*
                       History of the Oriental Arts
                       India: Paintings from Ajanta . . .
                       Marks and Mudras of the Buddha

Indonesian
  Borobudur . . .
  The Buddha:
    Temple Comples . . .
Japan
  Art and Spirit
  Arts of Japan . . .
  Buddhist Art
  Haiku
  Haiku: An Introduction . . .
  Japanese Calligraphy
  Nara and Kyoto . . .
  The Path
  Ryokan . . .
  Torches of Todaiji
  Woodblock Mandala . . .
Painting
  Arts of Japan . . .   *Ajanta . . .*
  In the Steps of the Buddha *The Arts of Japan*
  Tibetan Heritage   *Ceylon—Paintings . . .*
  Zen in Ryoko-in   *Himalayan Art*
                       India: Paintings from Ajanta . . .
                       Japan: Ancient Buddhist Paintings
                       Japan—Shintoism and Buddhism
                       The Story of the Buddha . . .
                       Tibetan Art Set
                       Tibetan Buddhism

Sculpture
  The Buddha:
    Temple Complex . . .   *Ajanta . . .*
    Buddhist Art   *L'Art Khmer*
    Gautama the Buddha   *The Art of Tibet*
    The Glory That Remains   *The Arts of Japan*
    Horyuji Temple   *Buddhism*
    Immortal Stupa   *Early Buddhist Art . . .*
    Nara, Japan   *Evolution of the Buddha Image*
    Thai Images of the Buddha   *The Great Stupa at Sanchi*
    Yakushiji Temple . . .   *Himalayan Art*
                                   History of the Oriental Arts
                                   Japan—Shinto and Buddhism
                                   Korean Religion
                                   Marks and Mudras of the Buddha
                                   Sanchi
                                   Tibetan Art Set
                                   Tibetan Buddhism

Sri Lanka
  Buddhism: Footprint of
    the Buddha . . .   *Ceylon—Paintings . . .*
  In the Steps of the Buddha
Thai
  Thai Images of the Buddha   *Marks and Mudras of the Buddha*
                                  The Story of the Buddha . . .

Zen
  Buddhism: Land of the   *The Arts of Japan*
    Disappearing Buddha . . .
  Spirit of Zen   *Japan—Shinto and Buddhism*
  Zen in Ryoko-in   *Philosophy of Zen*
                                  Zen

ASHOKA PILLARS
  The Glory That Remains   *Early Buddhist Art . . .*
                                  History of the Oriental Arts
AVALOKITESHVARA (*see also* **DALAI LAMA**)
  The Lama King
  The Spider's Thread
BEGGING (*see* **ALMS-GIVING/ALMS-ROUNDS**)
BHIKKHU (*see* **MONASTIC LIFE**)
BHUTAN
  Bhutan . . .   *Music of the Bhutan (R)*
  A King Is Crowned   *Tibetan Buddhist Rites . . . (R)*
BODHGAYA
  Land of Enlightenment   *Early Buddhist Art . . .*
BODHISATTVA
  Awareness
  Buddhist Art
  Horyuji Temple
  Immortal Stupa
  Jizo Children's Festival

and Communism/Marxism
  Burma, Buddhism and
    Neutralism
  The Lama King
Historical survey of
  The Buddha in South Asia   *Buddhism*
  Buddhism (Great Religions   *Buddhism in Southeast Asia . . .*
    Series)
  Buddhism in China   *The Buddhist Tradition. . . Burma*
  Buddhist Art   *The Buddhist Tradition . . . Japan*
  The Buddhist World   *Chinese Religions*
  Himalayan Buddhism   *Himalayan Art*
  Theravada Buddhism   *Japan—Shinto and Buddhism*
                      Korean Religion
                      Marks and Mudras of the Buddha
                      The World's Great Religions . . .

Spiritual discipline
  Buddhism: Be Ye Lamps . . .
  Buddhism: Footprint of
    the Buddha . . .
  Buddhism: Land of the
    Disappearing Buddha . . .
  Buddhism: The Path . . .
  I Am a Monk
  The Smile
  Vejen
  Zen in Life
  Zen in Ryoko-in   *The Way of Eheiji (R)*
Teachings
  Awareness
  The Buddha
  Buddhism (Great Religions
    Series)
  Buddhism: Be Ye Lamps . . .
  Buddhism: Footprint of
    the Buddha . . .
  Gautama the Buddha
  Meditation

BURMA
  Burma, Buddhism, and   *The Buddhist Tradition. . . Burma*
    Neutralism
  The Smile
  Vejen

CALLIGRAPHY
  Japanese Calligraphy

CAMBODIA
  Angkor Wat: The Lost City   *L'Art Khmer*
  Angkor Wat: The Ancient City *The Music of Cambodia (R)*

CAVE TEMPLES
  China
    Buddhism in China
    China: The Golden Age
  India
    Cave Temples of India—   *Ajanta . . .*
    Buddhist   *Ceylon—Paintings . . .*
                  India: Paintings from Ajanta . . .

HEALING (*see* MEDICINE)
HELL
    The Spider's Thread   *Tibetan Buddhism*
    Tibetan Heritage
HERBS/HERBAL MEDICINE
    I Am a Monk
HIMALAYA (*see* BHUTAN;
NEPAL; TIBET/TIBETAN)
    Bhutan   *The Art of Tibet*
    Himalayan Buddhism   *Buddhism*
    A King Is Crowned   *Himalayan Art*
    Out of This World . . .   *The Music of Tibetan Buddhism (R)*
    Sacred Art of Tibet   *Tibetan Art Set*
    Sherpa High Country   *Tibetan Buddhism*
    The Tantric Universe   *Tibetan Buddhism . . . (R)*
    Tibetan Heritage   *Tibetan Buddhist Rites (R)*
                              Tibetan Mystic Song (R)
                              Tibetan Songs . . . (R)
HINDU-BUDDHIST INTERACTION
    Angkor Wat: The Lost City
    Angkor Wat: The Ancient City
    The Buddha in South Asia
    Land of Enlightenment
    Nagarjunakonda
    Pearl of the East
    The Tantric Universe
HISTORICAL SURVEYS (*see* geographical entires; CHINA/CHINESE;
HIMALAYA: INDIA: JAPAN/JAPANESE; etc.)
HORYUJI (*see* TEMPLES)
ICONOGRAPHY
  Cross-cultural
    Buddhist Art   *Evolution of the Buddha Image*
                              Marks and Mudras of the Buddha
  Himalayan
    The Lama King
    Meditation Crystallized
    Sacred Art of Tibet
    Tantra of Gyuto   *Tibetan Art Set*
  Indian
    Gautama and Buddha   *India: Paintings from Ajanta Caves*
    The Glory That Remains
    Immortal Stupa
    Land of Enlightenment
    Nagarajunakonda
    Nalanda
  Japanese
    Horyuji Temple   *The Arts of Japan*
    Nara, Japan   *Japan - Shinto and Buddhism*
    Smiling Images of the Buddha
    Yakushiji Temple . . .
  Southeast Asia
    Angkor Wat: The Lost City   *L' Art Khmer*
    Angkor Wat: The Ancient City *Buddhism in Southeast Asia . . .*
    Borobudur . . .   *Story of the Buddha . . .*
    Thai Images of the Buddha

INDIA
Art (*see* ART[S]-Indian)
Buddhism
The Buddha in South Asia   *Ajanta . . .*
The Glory That Remains   *Buddhism*
Immortal Stupa   *Early Buddhist Art . . .*
Land of Enlightenment   *The Great Stupa of Sanchi*
Nagarajunakonda   *Sanchi*
Nalanda
Cave temples

                                  Ajanta . . .

INDONESIAN
Borobudur . . .   *Buddhism in Southeast Asia . . .*

JAPAN/JAPANESE
Aesthetics (*see* AESTHETICS)
Architecture
  (*see* ARCHITECTURE)
Art(s) (*see* ART[S]-Japanese)
Buddhism (*see* list of films
  under Buddhism-Japan)
                                  The Arts of Japan
                                  The Buddhist Tradition . . .Japan
                                  Buddhism in Japan `
                                  Japan - Shintoism and Buddhism
                                  Philosophy of Zen
                                  Zen
Contemporary
  Buddhism: Land of the
    Disappearing Buddha . . .
  Japan: Land of the Kami
  Japan: The Living
    Tradition . . .(I)
  The Spider's Thread
Dance (*see* DANCE, DRAMA, AND PERFORMING ARTS)
Drama (*see* DANCE, DRAMA, AND PERFORMING ARTS)
Folk Buddhism
  Buddhism and Shintoism . . .
  The Gods of Japan
Haiku (*see* poetry)
History and civilization
  Japan: Land of the Kami
  Japan: The Living
    Tradition . . . (II)
Iconography (*see* ICONOGRAPHY)
Lay/popular religion
  Buddhism and Shintoism . . .
  Buddhism: Land of the
    Disappearing Buddha . . .
  Japan: The Living
    Tradition . . . (I)
  Jizo Children s Festival
  Zen in Life
Mahayana
  Buddhism and Shintoism . . .

LAMA/LAMAISM

The Lama King
Out of This World
A Prophecy
Sherpa Legend
Tantra of Gyuto
The Tantric Universe
Tibetan Heritage

The Music of Tibetan Buddhism (R)
Tibetan Buddhism
Tibetan Buddhist Rites . . . (R)

LAY/MONK INTERACTION (*see* MONK/LAITY INTERACTION)

LAY/POPULAR RELIGION (*see also* FOLK BUDDHISM; FESTIVAL[S])
Chinese

Chinese Religions

Himalayan
A King Is Crowned
The Lama King
A Prophecy
Sherpa High Country
Tibetan Medicine . . .
Japanese
Buddhism and Shintoism . . .

*Buddhism: Land of the
Disappearing Buddha . . .*
Hiraizumi
*Japan: The Living
Tradition . . . (I)*
Jizo Children's Festival
Korean

Korean Religion

Sri Lanka
*Buddhism: Footprint of
the Buddha . . .*
Vesak
Thailand
Chiang Mai . . .

Buddhism in Southeast Asia . . .

MAHAYANA
*Buddhism (Great Religions
Series)*
Mahayana Buddhism
in China
Buddhism in China
in the Himalayas
Himalayan Buddhism
in Japan
*Japan: The Living
Tradition . . . (II)*
in Korea

The Buddhist Tradition . . . Japan
Japan-Shintoism and Buddhism

Korean Religion

in South Asia
Buddhism in South Asia
Nagarjunakonda
Nalanda
in Southeast Asia
Borobudur . . .

Buddhism

Buddhism in Southeast Asia . . .

MAITREYA
   Awareness
MANDALA
   The Lama King   *Tibetan Art Set*
   Meditation Crystallized   *Tibetan Buddhism*
   Tantra of Gyuto
MEDICINE
   I Am a Monk
   Tibetan Medicine . . .
MEDITATION
   Art of Meditation
   Buddhism: Footprint of   *Buddhist Chant (R)*
      the Buddha . . .
   Buddhism: Land of the   *Tibetan Buddhism . . . (R)*
   Disappearing Buddha . . .
   I Am a Monk   *Tibetan Buddhist Rites . . . (R)*
   The Lama King   *The Way of Eheiji (R)*
   Theravada Buddhism   *Zen*
   Zen in Life
   Zen Training of a Young Monk
MERIT (*see also* MONK/LAITY INTERACTION)
   Buddhism: Be Ye Lamps . . .   *Buddhism in Southeast Asia . . .*
   Buddhism: Footprint of   *The Buddhist Tradition . . . Burma*
      the Buddha . . .
MONASTIC LIFE
   Buddhism: Be Ye Lamps . . .   *Buddhism in Southeast Asia . . .*
   Buddhism: Footprint of   *Buddhist Chant (R)*
      the Buddha . . .
                                        The Buddhist Tradition. . . Burma
   I Am a Monk   *The Buddhist Tradition . . . Japan*
   The Religious Investiture . . .   *Chinese Religions*
   The Lama King   *Himalayan Art*
   Nalanda   *Korean Religion*
   A Prophecy   *Monk's Ordination Ceremony*
   Requiem for a Faith   *Music of Japan IV . . . (R)*
   The Smile   *The Music of Tibetan Buddhism (R)*
   Temple of the Twenty Pagodas   *Religious Music of Asia (R)*
   Tibetan Heritage   *Tibetan Buddhism . . . (R)*
   Vejen   *Tibetan Buddhist Rites . . . (R)*
   Zen Facets of Japanese Religion   *Tibetan Songs . . . (R)*
   Zen in Life   *The Way of Eheiji (R)*
   Zen in Ryoko-in   *Zen*
MONASTIC TRAINING
   Chinese
                                        Chinese Religions
   Japanese
   Buddhism: Land of the   *The Way of Eheiji (R)*
      Disappearing Buddha . . .   *Zen*
   Japan: The Living   *The Way of Eheiji (R)*
      Tradition . . .(I)
   Zen Facets of Japanese Religion   *Zen*
   Zen in Life
   Zen Training of a Young Monk
   Thai
   Temple of the Twenty Pagodas   *Monk's Ordination Ceremony*
   Thailand

Tibetan
  The Religious Investiture . . .
  A Prophecy
  Tibetan Heritage

MONK/LAITY INTERACTION (*see also* ALMS-GIVING/ALMS-ROUNDS)
  Buddhism: Be Ye Lamps . . .   *Buddhism in Southeast Asia . . .*
  Buddhism: Footprint of   *Chinese Religions*
    the Buddha
  Chiang Mai . . .
  A King Is Crowned
  The Lama King   *The Music of Tibetan Buddhism (R)*
  A Prophecy
  The Smile
  Temple of the Twenty Pagodas   *Tibetan Buddhist Rites . . . (R)*
  Thailand
  Zen in Life

MUSIC
  Buddhist Dances of Korea
  Lama Dances of Tibet
  Sherpa High Country
  Tantra of Gyuto

NAGARJUNAKONDA
  Nagarjunakonda

NALANDA
  Nalanda

NARA
  Horyuji Temple   *The Arts of Japan*
  Nara and Kyoto . . .   *Japan-Shinto and Buddhism*
  Nara, Japan   *Nara and Kyoto*
  Torches of Todaiji

NATIONALISM (*see also* RELIGION AND THE STATE)
  Burma, Buddhism and
    Neutralism
  Japan: The Living
    Tradition (I)
  Thailand

NATURE
  Art of Meditation
  Awareness
  Buddhism, Man and Nature
  Flow of Zen
  Haiku
  Haiku: An Introduction . . .
  Japan: Land of the Kami
  Mood of Zen
  The Smile
  Vejen
  Zen and Now

NEPAL
  Sherpa High Country   *The Art of Tibet*
  Sherpa Legend   *Himalayan Buddhism*
  The Tantric Universe
  Tibetan Heritage

NEW RELIGIONS OF JAPAN
  Art and Spirit
  Japan: Land of the Kami
  Japan: The Living
    Tradition . . . (I)
NICHIREN BUDDHISM
  The Gods of Japan   *The Buddhist Tradition . . . Japan*
  Japan: The Living
    Tradition . . . (II)
  Zen Facets of Japanese Religion
NICHIREN SHOSHU ACADEMY
  New York Convention—1976
  Pre-Bicentennial
    Convention . . .
NOH DRAMA (*see under* DANCE, DRAMA, AND PERFORMING ARTS)
NOVITIATE (*see* MONASTIC TRAINING)
ORDINATION (*see* MONASTIC TRAINING)
PADMASAMBHAVA
  A King Is Crowned   *The Music of Tibetan Buddhism (R)*
  Lama Dances of Tibet   *Tibetan Buddhism . . . (R)*
                                         Tibetan Buddhist Rites . . . (R)
PAGODA (*see* STUPA; TEMPLES)
PAINTING (*see* ART[S])
PERFORMING ARTS (*see* DANCE, DRAMA, AND PERFORMING ARTS)
PILGRIMAGE AND PILGRIMAGE SITES (*see also* RITUAL)
  Borobudur . . .   *Buddhism in Southeast Asia . . .*
  Buddhism: The Path . . .   *Early Buddhist Art . . .*
  Honorable Mountain   *Korean Religion*
  Immortal Stupa
  In the Steps of the Buddha
  Land of Enlightenment
  Meditation
  Song of Ceylon
POETRY
  Haiku
  Haiku: An Introduction . . .
  Ryokan . . .   *Tibetan Mystic Song (R)*
  Zen in Ryoko-in   *Tibetan Songs . . .*
POLONARUVA
  Buddhism: The Path . . .   *Buddhism in Southeast Asia . . .*
  Song of Ceylon   *Ceylon—Paintings . . .*
POPULAR RELIGION (*see* LAY/POPULAR RELIGION;
FOLK BUDDHISM)
POTTERY (*see also* ART[S]; CRAFTS)
  Art and Spirit
  Arts of Japan . . .
  Spirit of Zen
PURE LAND BUDDHISM
  Buddhism and Shintoism . . .   *The Buddhist Tradition . . . Japan*
  Buddhism: Land of the
    Disappearing Buddha . . .
  The Gods of Japan
  Japan: The Living
    Tradition . . . (II)
RELIGION AND THE STATE (*see also* NATIONALISM)
  Bhutan . . .
  Buddhism: Footprint of
    the Buddha . . .

TEMPLES (*see also* ARCHITECTURE; CAVE TEMPLES; STUPA)
Japan
   Buddhist Art   *The Arts of Japan*
   Hiraizumi . . .   *The Buddhist*
   Horyuji Temple   *Tradition . . . Japan*
                                   Japan—Shinto nd Buddhism
   Nara and Kyoto . . .   *The Way of Eheiji (R)*
   Restoration of the
     Golden Shrine
   Torches of Todaiji
   Yakushiji Temple . . .
   Zen in Life   *Zen*
   Zen in Ryoko-in
Pagoda
   Temple of the Twenty Pagodas
   Vejen
   Yakushiji Temple
Thai
   Temple of the Twenty Pagodas   *Buddhism in Southeast Asia . . .*
Tibetan
   Out of This World . . . .   *Himalayan Art*
                                   Tibetan Buddhism
                                   Tibetan Buddhist Rites . . . (R)

TENDAI BUDDHISM
   Japan: Land of the Kami   *Japan-Shinto and Buddhism*
   Japan: The Living
     Tradition . . . (II)
THAILAND
   Buddhism: Be Ye Lamps . . .   *Buddhism in Southeast Asia . . .*
   Chiang Mai . . .   *Monk's Ordination Ceremony*
   I Am a Monk   *The Story of the Buddha . . .*
   Temple of the Twenty Pagodas
   Thai Images of the Buddha
   Thailand
   Thailand: Land of Smiles
THERAVADA
   The Buddha in South Asia   *Buddha and His Teachings*
   Buddhism   *Buddhism*
   Buddhism: Be Ye Lamps . . .   *Buddhism in Southeast Asia . . .*
   Buddhism: The Path . . .   *The Buddhist*
   Chiang Mai . . .   *Tradition . . . Burma*
   I Am a Monk   *The Story of the Buddha . . .*
   In the Steps of the Buddha
   Meditation   *Monk's Ordination Ceremony*
   Song of Ceylon
   Temple of the Twenty Pagodas
   Theravada Buddhism
   Vejen
TIBET/TIBETAN (*see also* ARCHITECTURE-Himalayan; DALAI
LAMA; HIMALAYA)
Buddhism
   The Lama King
   A Prophecy
   Out of This World . . .   *The Art of Tibet*
   Requiem for a Faith   *Himalayan Art*
   Sacred Art of Tibet   *The Music of Tibetan Buddhism (R)*
                                 Tibetan Art Set

Sherpa Legend
Tantra of Gyuto
The Tantric Universe
Tibetan Heritage

Exile
The Lama King
A Prophecy
Requiem for a Faith
Tantra of Gyuto
Tibetan Story
History and civilization
Himalayan Buddhism
Out of This World . . .
Tibetan Heritage
Symbolism
Meditation Crystallized
Requiem for a Faith
Sacred Art of Tibet
Temples
Out of This World . . .
TODAIJI (*see* TEMPLES)
URBAN RELIGION
Japan: Land of the Kami
Japan: The Living
Tradition . . . (I)
Jizo Children's Festival
Vesak
VAJRAYANA (*see also* TANTRA)
The Buddha in South Asia
Buddhism in China
Himalayan Buddhism
Meditation Crystallized
Sherpa Legend
Tantra of Gyuto
The Tantric Universe
Tibetan Heritage
VESAK (*see also* BUDDHA(S)-Shakyamuni, life of)
Vesak
VESSANTARA (*see* BODHISATTVA)
WORSHIP (*see also* RITUAL)
Borobudur . . .
The Tantric Universe
Temple of the Twenty Pagodas
Theravada Buddhism
Tibetan Heritage
ZEN (*see also* JAPAN/JAPANESE)
aesthetics
Gen . . .
The Path
Spirit of Zen
Zen in Ryoko-in
American (*see also* AMERICAN BUDDHISM)
Zen in America
Archery
Kyudo . . .

Tibetan Buddhism
Tibetan Buddhism . . . (R)
Tibetan Buddhist Rites . . . (R)
Tibetan Mystic Song (R)
Tibetan Songs . . . (R)

Tibetan Buddhism

Himalayan Art
Tibetan Art Set
Tibetan Buddhism

Tibetan Buddhism

Buddhism in Southeast Asia . . .

Chinese Religions

Tibetan Buddhism

Chinese Religions
The Music of Tibetan Buddhism (R)
Tibetan Mystic Song (R)

The Arts of Japan
Philosophy of Zen
Zen

Art(s)
  Buddhism: Land of the   *The Arts of Japan*
    Disappearing Buddha . . .   *Japan-Shinto and Buddhism*
  Japanese Calligraphy
  The Path
  Ryokan . . .
  Spirit of Zen
Chinese (Ch'an)
  Buddhism in China
Garden
  Mood of Zen
Laity
  Zen in Ryoko-in
Meditation
  Buddhism: Land of the   *Philosophy of Zen*
    Disappearing Buddha . . .   *The Way of Eheiji (R)*
  Zen Training of a Young Monk   *Zen*
Monastic life (*see* MONASTIC LIFE; MONASTIC TRAINING)
Nature and Zen
  Flow of Zen   *Philosophy of Zen*
  Mood of Zen
  Zen and Now
Rinzai
  Zen in Ryoko-in
Soto
  Zen in Life   *Zen*
Taoism and
  Flow of Zen
  Mood of Zen
Temples
  Zen in Life   *Japan—Shinto and Buddhism*
  Zen in Ryoko-in   *The Way of Eheiji (R)*
                           Zen

Films Generally Not Available

Buddhism—A Question of Conscience
Cambodia: The Angkor Mystery
Daibutsu
Faith of the Buddha
Gateway to the Gods (Japan only)
Golden Temple, Silver Temple
In Quest of Japanese Thoughts:
Ryokan's Snow, Moon and Flowers
(UNIJAP)

Kyoto: Zen Buddhism
Land of the Buddha
Nirvana
Order of the Yellow Robe
People of the Buddha
Shinran Shonin: Footsteps in
the Snowstorm

Forthcoming Films
(Films not ready for review as of
November 1979)

Open University
Mindful Way (1980)
Roaring Silence (1980)
Thread Cross Films
A Trilogy on Tibet: Radiating the
Fruit of Truth (1980)
A Trilogy on Tibet: The Fields of the
Senses (1980) (see review of the first
film in this trilogy: *A Prophecy*)

University of Wisconsin
Buddhist Doctrine: Wheel of
Light (1980)
Buddhist Monastic Life and
Education in Tibet (1980)
Buddhist Teachings and
Practices and Tibetan Laity
(projected 1981)

JAPAN FOUNDATION (Washington, D.C.)
Zen Culture, Zen Spirit (1980)
Zen Temple—Eiheiji (1980)

ALPHABETICAL LISTING OF MATERIALS REVIEWED

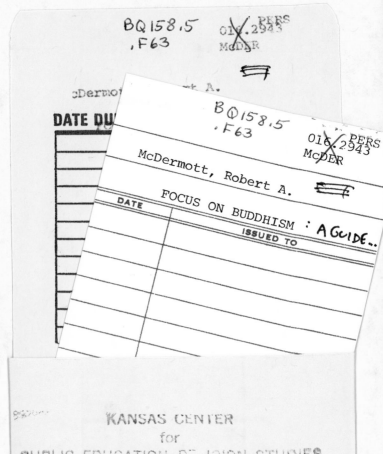